MICROWAVE
RECIPES
FOR ONE

Other cookery titles from Elliot Right Way Books:

How To Boil An Egg . . . And 184 Other Simple Recipes
   For One
Food Processors Properly Explained
Slow Cooking Properly Explained
Pressure Cooking Properly Explained
The Stir Fry Cook
An Indian Housewife's Recipe Book
The Curry Secret

By the same author:

Microwave Cooking Properly Explained
Out Of The Freezer Into The Microwave
The Microwave Planner – How To Adapt Your Family
   Favourites
The Barbecue Cook

Front Cover
Recipe: Salmon with Cucumber Sauce (page 52)
Photographer: Michael Kay, Solar Studios, Croydon
Microwave cooker supplied by: Samsung Electronics (UK) Ltd
Home Economist: Annette Yates

MICROWAVE RECIPES FOR ONE

Annette Yates

RIGHT WAY

Typeset in 11/12pt Times by County Typesetters, Margate, Kent.

Printed and bound in Great Britain by Cox & Wyman Ltd., Reading, Berkshire.

The *Right Way* series and the *Paperfronts* series are both published by Elliot Right Way Books, Brighton Road, Lower Kingswood, Tadworth, Surrey, KT20 6TD, U.K.

CONTENTS

ACKNOWLEDGEMENTS

The author would like to record her thanks to the following companies.

For the loan of microwave cookers for recipe testing:

Samsung Electronics (UK) Ltd, 225 Hook Rise South, Surbiton, Surrey KT6 7LD.

Sharp Electronics, Sharp House, Thorp Road, Manchester M10 9BE.

Toshiba (UK) Ltd, Toshiba House, Frimley Road, Frimley, Camberley, Surrey GU16 5JJ.

For equipment and wrappings:

Lakeland Plastics, Alexandra Buildings, Station Precinct, Windermere, Cumbria LA23 1BQ.

Newell UK Ltd, Unit 21, Eyncourt Road, Woodside Estate, Dunstable, Bedfordshire LU5 4TS.

Terinex Ltd, Elms Industrial Estate, Bedford MK41 0ND.

This book is dedicated to my daughters, Emma and Lindsay, who always appreciate my 'work'.

INTRODUCTION

Here is my contribution to those of you who have to cook for one. I refer not only to those of you who live alone, but also to those who cook for one for any other reason. Perhaps you are a student, cooking for yourself. Maybe members of your family need to eat at different times? Maybe someone is on a special diet which requires food to be cooked separately? Maybe members of your household have tastes and preferences which differ greatly – perhaps one of you is vegetarian? Then, of course, there are always the occasions when you are alone at a mealtime – lunch-time is a good example where I am concerned. It is this type of occasion when you (or I) may be tempted to fall into bad eating habits which in turn can result in a monotonous, unvaried diet of snacks. Taking a little time to care for *yourself* on these occasions will, I am sure, give you feelings of satisfaction and well-being.

This book aims to cut down time-consuming planning and cooking methods to a minimum – leaving you either with more time to live the rest of your busy life or, like me, with more time in the kitchen to enjoy being creative with food. With the help of this book, you will find cooking for one easier, more fun, and not necessarily more expensive than cooking for several.

So often I am asked for cooking times for one portion or one item. 'Most recipes seem to be geared to four people!' you complain. 'Is there a simple rule of thumb which enables me to cut the cooking time according to the quantity?' you ask. In answer to the first question, cookery writers are now becoming aware of the large percentage of readers needing recipes and times for one.

The answer to the second question is 'No'. There are however simple guidelines, on page 29, which will help to build up your knowledge and, more importantly, your confidence when dealing with small quantities. There are also in this book over 85 tested recipes and ideas for quick, nutritious dishes using convenient ingredients. Many of the recipes have been acquired during micro-wave classes and demonstrations over the years. Every recipe involves *cooking* and not simply marrying two or three 'convenience' foods to make a meal. They have been written for those who are *interested* in what they eat. They are for those who are *interested* in making sure that their diet is varied, exciting, and provides the nutrients needed for a healthy lifestyle – without the slavery to the kitchen!

The subjects of thawing and reheating are given greater emphasis in 'Out Of The Freezer Into The Microwave'. Similarly, 'Microwave Cooking Properly Explained' and 'The Microwave Planner' concentrate on giving infor-mation about the workings of the microwave cooker and adapting everyday recipes, together with plenty of recipes.

Finally, in addition to the recipes in this book you will no doubt have your own favourite dishes in mind. Do try them out – you won't know how good they are until you do. Doubtless you will make some mistakes (I know I do) but don't give up, learn from them, look at them as a challenge, and soon your confidence and your success rate will soar!

Annette Yates

1

WHAT ARE THE ADVANTAGES?

Speed
Whether you are cooking for one or for six the main advantage of microwave cooking will always be speed. In general, conventional cooking times can be cut by 60–75%. A chicken portion takes less than 5 minutes, a potato in its jacket takes 4–6 minutes, and a one-portion sponge pudding takes just 2 minutes – to name but a few examples.

Cost
In terms of fuel savings you cannot beat the microwave. It uses only about one quarter of the power required to run a conventional oven, and cooking times are dramatically shorter. The microwave energy is directed straight into the food – none is wasted heating up the containers or the

walls of the cavity. In addition, the lower the power level used, the less electricity is used. Finally, there is very little loss of heat from the tightly-sealed unit of a microwave cooker.

Versatility

There are very few foods which cannot be thawed, cooked or reheated in the microwave, though there will always be some foods which personal taste will tell you to cook conventionally. As you will see in the recipe pages the possibilities are endless.

Remember, though, that the microwave will not cook eggs in their shells (for making boiled egg), batter-coated foods, toast, pies, crusty bread and pancakes. Deep-fat frying should never be attempted in the microwave, and boiling more than 600ml (1 pt) water is usually quicker and more economical using the electric kettle.

A microwave cooker is ideal for cooking small quantities of food, though it will cope very well with large amounts when necessary too.

Food can be prepared in advance and reheated or (probably more likely when you are cooking for one) cooked as and when it is needed. Since the microwave cooks in the shortest possible time and in the minimum amount of liquid, the maximum nutritional content is retained. It also copes easily with low-fat cooking (see page 24).

Space-saving

If you have a small kitchen or a restricted area in which to prepare food, the microwave takes up a proportionally small space. This makes it very suitable for use in bedsits too. Microwave cooker sizes vary tremendously today, so you should always be able to find a model to suit your individual needs (see page 12).

Ease Of Use

A microwave cooker can be plugged in anywhere there is

a 13 amp socket. It can therefore be moved about (see page 13) when necessary. The complexity of controls varies from model to model, depending on its features. Once learned, however, they are simple. There are many models which incorporate just a few controls (adequate for most requirements: pages 13–15) and most people find them easy to use. This makes them particularly suitable for the elderly or the disabled – in fact anyone who has to look after themselves.

Clean In Use

Food can be cooked and served in the same dish, and drinks can be heated in the cup or mug. In microwave cookers there is no direct heat to bake or burn foods on to the containers, so washing-up is cut to a minimum. Oven cleaning is easy too. Similarly, since there is no direct heat to burn on spillages (as in a conventional oven) the oven walls are easily cleaned with a damp cloth. Finally you will find fewer cooking smells, less steam, and your kitchen-cooking area remains cool.

Combination cookers (see page 14) do tend to get more soiled than microwave-only cookers, because the oven walls heat up (and therefore food splashes can bake on). Using microwave or roasting bags (see page 18) helps reduce soiling by preventing splashes from reaching the hot oven walls.

2

WHICH MICROWAVE TO CHOOSE?

If you have yet to purchase your first microwave cooker, or if you are updating your model, you may be rather awed by the prospect that there are hundreds of models from which to choose. If you are updating your present model your task will be easier since you will already be aware of any shortfalls in your existing oven. To help you whittle your choice down to just a few models, I have devised some questions which you may like to ask yourself while looking at microwave features. I am sure that they will also stimulate you to think of extra questions relating to your own particular needs.

1. How much space do you have and where? If you cook for one person (i.e. yourself) on a permanent basis, this is probably the first question you will ask yourself.

There are many compact models available which take up the minimum space on a worktop or shelf. Some can be fixed on the wall. Check these small models carefully though if you require more than the most basic functions and wattage. Whatever size or wattage you choose, the oven will need to be positioned near a 13 amp socket outlet. All microwave cookers have vents, so check where these are positioned. Allow an area for ventilation of 5–8cm (2–3 in) all round. You will also need sufficient clearance to open the door, with an area of work surface nearby on which to set down hot dishes. Maybe you will want the oven to be built in to your kitchen – if so, check that it is suitable for this and whether there is extra cost involved.

2. How much do you want to pay? Normally this question would come top of the list, but the assumption that you will probably require a table-top version cuts down the range of prices anyway. Begin by looking in the medium price range – most cookers here should suit your basic requirements.

3. Will you want to move the microwave around? Maybe you will want to move it from one room to another, or perhaps outside. Maybe you will want to take it with you on self-catering holidays. These points will dictate the exterior size of the oven and its weight too. Some table-top models can be very heavy. You will notice that all cookers are heavier on one side – usually the side containing the microwave-making valve (the magnetron).

4. How do you intend to use your microwave? Look at the type of life you lead and the sort of food you eat. Will you be using it to cook? If so, then you will probably require one with variable controls. Are you likely to be preparing food in advance? Some models incorporate advance programming, enabling the

microwaves to switch on while you are out. Some will keep your food warm on a heat-and-hold program. On the other hand, if you are likely to be doing much less cooking and more thawing and reheating, a fairly basic machine will suit you. Look at the specifications on every model you view. Wattages vary from 500 to 1000. Many recipes (and certainly all mine) are developed on 600–700W machines. Microwave cooking on a 500W machine will still be faster than conventional cooking, but if speed really is of the essence (and we all seem to get busier by the day!) then you may become frustrated with a lower wattage. See page 29 for details on adjusting cooking times. Finally, if you prepare and cook a lot of pastry or roast dishes you may like to consider buying a combination oven (see number 7 below).

5. Are you likely to be cooking for more than one person in the future? Do you entertain often? If the answer to either of these questions is 'yes' you should look at purchasing a microwave cooker with a slightly larger oven capacity than you need at present. Do not be misled by first appearances. Open the door and look at the inner cavity. Check whether it will take larger containers and larger items of food (a large chicken or a large casserole, for example).

6. Do you already have an efficient grill? If not, look at those models which incorporate a browning element or grill. Check whether it will cook small pieces of meat or fish, or whether it is suitable for simply browning the tops of dishes.

7. Are you replacing a conventional oven? Space may be limited. Perhaps you do not have a conventional oven at present and do not wish (or have the resources) to purchase two cooking appliances. There are many combination ovens on the market now. They are

generally more expensive and can be slightly larger than most microwave ovens. They combine convection, microwave and radiant heat in the one appliance – in other words you can use them as a microwave, as a conventional oven, or a combination of both. The oven cavity is smaller than a conventional oven, making them particularly suitable for cooking for one or two. Many models have a grill and some have a rotisserie attachment.

8. Do you have the time to learn new processes? I have spoken to people who, in updating their microwave, have chosen the more complex models. You may be told that they take the thinking out of microwave cooking – with automatic sensors doing everything bar washing the dishes! Many of these people had been perfectly happy with their former models but were now having difficulties. A common complaint was that pre-set programs (some models have 20 or so) using the automatic sensor were not cooking food to their liking. I have stressed in previous books that the degree to which food is cooked must be left to personal taste and preference. So if you are buying a microwave cooker for the first time, consider carefully before buying a very sophisticated model. This is not underestimating your intelligence, but in my experience it takes far longer to learn, and to gain confidence in, microwave cooking in a model which has an endless choice of programs. Despite this, if you do take the time to use and get to know these machines they usually prove to be indispensable.

9. Do you have problems in operating machines? Elderly or disabled readers will find that microwaving is a convenient and safe way to cook. There are many touch-control models available for ease of use, and for visually disabled persons, some manufacturers can supply braille panels.

3

THE NECESSARY
EQUIPMENT

Cooking Containers
Cooking containers are suitable if they allow the microwaves to pass straight through them into the food. Metal
containers should not be used for microwaving – the
microwaves are reflected off them and they could even
cause damage to your cooker. Plates and containers with
metal decorations should not be used since the decoration
will spark and blacken. Having advised against the use of
metal, it *is* permissible to use small areas of smooth foil to
shield delicate or thin areas of food, to prevent them from
overcooking. Always follow your manufacturer's instructions carefully regarding the use of foil, never allowing it
to touch the oven walls. (In combination cookers, when
cooking on convection or grill only, metal containers can
be used – just as in a conventional oven/grill.)

So what type of container is appropriate? Ovenglass, glass ceramic, pottery and stoneware are suitable for cooking and will withstand high temperatures as the food heats up. Paper, plastic, baskets, wood and cardboard should be used for short-term heating only. Use kitchen paper to absorb moisture and as a cover to prevent food from spitting or splashing on to the cavity walls.

A wide range of containers is on offer, which have been designed specifically for the microwave – in heat-resistant plastic, glass and ceramic. Many can be used in the microwave, in the freezer and in the conventional oven too. Always check with the label when you are buying equipment, to make sure it is most suitable for your day-to-day requirements. If you have a dishwasher it is worth checking that containers are dishwasher-proof too.

Checkpoints for containers
*   Round shapes arc best – the microwaves can reach all sides of the food evenly.

*   A ring shape is excellent for larger cakes, meat loaves and other foods which cannot be stirred during cooking. The slow-cooking centre, which is sometimes found when cooking in a normal round container, is not a problem.

*   Squares and rectangles are prone to overcooking at their corners.

*   A bowl has no corners and is most suitable for foods which need stirring during cooking.

*   Straight-sided containers produce better results than those with sloping sides.

Plastic Bags And Covers
Ordinary plastic bags should not be used in the micro-wave. It is sometimes suggested that frozen vegetables

can be cooked in their original wrapping. Small amounts of vegetables microwaved for short periods may be successful, but take care that the plastic does not melt. Do not use plastic dairy containers.

Microwave bags (and roasting bags)

These special bags are available in a range of sizes. They withstand high temperatures and are excellent for cooking single portions of fish, meat, vegetables, fruit and puddings. They are particularly useful for microwaving small quantities of soup, casseroles and for reheating plated meals. They can be used in the microwave, in the conventional oven (up to a specified temperature), as a boil-in-the-bag, and for freezer storage. When microwaving, sit the bag of food in a small, rigid container (to keep it an even, uniform shape) and tuck the open ends under loosely so that steam can escape.

Boil-in-the-bags

These are also resistant to high temperatures and are useful for single portions in the microwave, for boiling on the hob and for freezing. Some commercially frozen foods and pre-prepared products are supplied in these bags which make them ideal for microwave cooking. Always remember to make a small slit in the bag to prevent it ballooning up (and possibly bursting) and to allow the steam to escape.

Clear film

When no suitable lid is available, clear film is useful for covering dishes in the microwave. However, do not allow it to touch the food and do not be tempted to line dishes with it. Remember to pierce the film during microwave cooking to prevent it ballooning up and to allow steam to escape.

Other Useful Accessories

* Microwave rack. This helps food to cook evenly. It

lifts the food (particularly if it is unsuitable for stirring) off the base of the oven or turntable in order that the microwaves can reach underneath the container. It can also be used to cook foods which need draining and which are best kept out of their cooking juices, e.g. bacon rashers, chicken joints.

* Browning dish. Browning dishes have a special coating which reaches a high temperature when exposed to microwaves. Please note – this is the *only* type of container which should ever be put into the microwave *empty* when the microwaves are switched on. A browning dish is particularly useful for imitating shallow frying of meat, sausages, bacon, eggs and 'toasted' sandwiches. Do follow the manufacturer's instructions carefully.

* Small casserole with lid – preferably with straight, rather than sloping, sides.

* Kitchen paper. This is used under and on top of foods to absorb fat and moisture, and as a cover to prevent the cooker walls being splashed by spitting food.

* A jug for heating liquids and for making sauces. Even though you may be cooking small quantities, the liquid must have room to rise or boil up in the jug, so choose one larger than you would normally think necessary.

* Small bowls or ramekins for mixing very small amounts, for melting and for cooking.

* Small (600ml/1 pt) and medium (1.1 litre/2 pt) mixing bowls.

* A measuring jug, for accuracy.

* A set of measuring spoons, in metric, imperial, or both.

*   A small set of scales, also for accurate results.

*   Wooden spoon and a small hand whisk.

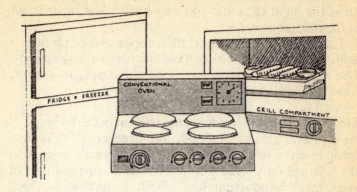

4

THE MICROWAVE'S PARTNERS

When cooking for one (or for two) you will probably find that certain kitchen appliances are invaluable partners to the microwave – making food preparation more convenient, speedy and fun. Sometimes they will help you to produce better results too.

The Refrigerator
This is an obvious partner to any type of cooking appliance and ensures that we can safely buy food days in advance of cooking it. Can you imagine the time and effort involved in shopping on a daily basis for quantities to serve one person? One point worth remembering at this stage is that all the recipes in this book (and indeed in most other cookery books) have been tested using ingredients at room temperature. So next time a recipe

takes a little longer to cook, consider the margarine, the milk, the meat etc., that you may have taken straight out of the refrigerator.

Today there are many chilled foods and ready meals available, many of which have microwave instructions. The microwave heating times on these are, of course, from chilled (i.e. straight out of the refrigerator).

The Freezer (or the freezer compartment in the fridge)

As I have always stressed, the freezer is a perfect companion to your microwave. It is no longer relegated to the 'storage only' area but it becomes an integral part of your meal 'production line'. With a microwave, food stored in the freezer is ready for immediate use. For speed and convenience, thaw frozen items in your microwave. Use your freezer to store extra portions of cooked food, cooked left-overs and everyday items such as bread rolls. Frozen vegetables, fruit, meat and fish are all assets to any microwave cook. Entire meals can then be thawed and cooked or reheated in the microwave in minutes.

It is encouraging to note how many frozen food manufacturers include microwave instructions on their products today, usually packaged in microwave-suitable containers to save us the chore of emptying food from a foil container.

The Grill

The grill is a very useful appliance – not just for making toast but also for finishing off many dishes to give them a crispy brown surface. A grilled surface provides instant appeal in terms of colour, aroma and flavour. Having an efficient grill also means that you can use it to cook foods such as sausages or chops while you prepare vegetables, rice, pasta or a sauce in the microwave. This can often halve the time spent in the kitchen.

The Hob

When microwaving for one, the hob can come in useful

for 'side-by-side' cooking too. For example, cooking the spaghetti on the hob, leaving the microwave free for preparing the bolognese sauce, or vice versa – again, saving time.

5

A WORD ABOUT
HEALTHY EATING

Over the last few years, hardly a day seems to have passed without some media comment on food and diet – telling us we should eat this and we shouldn't eat that. Whatever the reports (and these can often be conflicting) the basis of a healthy diet remains the same. A healthy diet is one which is balanced – providing us with sufficient of each of the nutrients our bodies need in order to live a healthy life, whether at work, rest or play. What *has* changed is the assessment of *how much* of each of the basic nutrients we actually need.

Years ago we would have been told that, in order to be fit and healthy (or indeed to lose weight), we should cut down on starchy foods like bread, potatoes, pasta and rice. Since then we have been advised that these foods are not actually the 'bad guys' but it is what we put *on* them that makes the difference. It is the rich sauces and lashings of cream, butter and other fats that are the culprits. Over the years, it seems that, with our improved lifestyles and an ever-expanding choice of foods, we as a nation have fallen into bad habits, eating too much of certain foods and not enough of others.

More recently, the diet experts have put together some definitive guidelines. In general, they tell us that the basis of our diet should be made up of 'complex carbohydrates' such as bread, potatoes, pasta, rice and pulses (peas, beans and lentils). At the same time we should limit our intake of fat (saturated fats in particular) and protein in the form of meat, fish, milk, eggs and cheese – which, incidentally, often contain fat. We are also urged to cut down on salt and sugar – not just the sugar we put in tea or coffee, or on breakfast cereals, but also sweets, chocolates and the hidden sugars to be found in ready-made drinks and other foods (many of which you might not expect to contain sugar). Finally, we should be eating five portions of fruit and vegetables a day – for plenty of fibre, vitamins and minerals.

Having looked at these recommendations, it is still my opinion that a balanced diet is best achieved by eating a *variety* of foods (particularly fresh foods) with *no excesses*.

Over the years we have seen improvements in food-labelling, all of which can help us in our choice of foods. Not only are ingredients being listed in more detail, but the labels on many foods now also contain nutritional information as well as cooking instructions (including microwave cooking instructions).

So how does the microwave fit into all this?

In general, microwaves cook fresh food in the least amount of liquid and in the shortest possible time. This way the food retains its maximum flavour, texture and nutritional value; vitamins and flavour are not washed out into copious quantities of cooking liquid. As a result, the flavour is concentrated, with less need to add extra salt.

Fish, meat, poultry and vegetables all cook well with

little or no liquid in the microwave. Because microwaving is essentially a moist method of cooking, we can also omit the fat usually used in a conventional recipe, e.g. when softening vegetables for a soup, sauce or casserole.

While cooking for one it can be tempting to rely on the frying pan and ready-prepared foods. Now, with the help of the microwave you can easily switch to a healthier diet. It is also compact, convenient, safe, and easy to use – making it highly suitable for young people and the elderly.

Home-made soups, sauces, fish, vegetable and meat dishes, rice, pasta, and desserts need no longer be a chore when cooking for one – as the recipe pages show.

Thawing takes only minutes so you no longer have to worry if you forget to take an item out of the freezer. Snacks need no longer be made up of crisps, biscuits or chocolate. The microwave can help you to make healthy snacks in no time at all.

Reheating is no longer the chore it used to be. The microwave reheats food quickly and efficiently, often improving the flavour and texture of foods such as vegetables, casseroles and sauces. It is particularly good at reheating small portions (i.e. for one) – and it is economical too.

With all these points in mind I have no doubt that, with the microwave, you will need to do far less thinking about, and planning for, a healthy diet. It is likely to come naturally!

6

USING THE RECIPES

The recipes in this book have been developed and tested by microwave only, so no matter which type of microwave cooker you have in your kitchen, you will be able to cook these dishes. There are one or two recipes which benefit from the use of a grill – if your microwave has a grill then do use it. What you will not find in these pages are recipes for combination cooking. Since each combination cooker differs from the next, it is difficult to cover everything in one book. However, you can be sure that your microwave will successfully cook every recipe in 'Microwave Recipes For One'.

Stirring And Turning Food In The Microwave
Foods cooked in the microwave need to be turned and/or stirred to encourage even cooking. The recipe methods have included instructions for this where necessary.

Covering Food In The Microwave

Many foods need to be covered in the microwave. This is particularly relevant when cooking small quantities of food which can easily dry out.

Always use appropriate-sized containers which suit the quantity of food being cooked. For example, do not try and cook a small amount of soup in a very large casserole – the large surface area will cause excess evaporation and you will be left with very little soup. On the other hand, the container does need to be large enough to allow the soup to boil up.

So when do you cover food? When you want to keep moisture in (e.g. soups, sauces, casseroles, vegetables, puddings) cover with a lid or pierced clear film (see page 18). When retention of moisture would spoil the dish (e.g. reheating pastry dishes) or when it would make it too watery (e.g. cooking the sauce around the Honeyed Spare Ribs on page 72) leave it uncovered. If you are undecided whether to cover or not, then it probably doesn't matter! The recipes in the following pages include instructions for covering within the methods. Where no cover is mentioned, none is used.

Cooking Times

All recipes in this book have been tested on 600–700W microwave cookers.

If your microwave has a lower wattage
*   add on about 20 seconds for each minute (for instance, 3 minutes in a 600–700W model should be extended to about 4 minutes in a lower-wattage cooker). In other words, add on about one third of the cooking time.

If your microwave has a higher wattage, *either*
*   deduct about 15 seconds for each minute (for instance, 3 minutes in a 600–700W model should be reduced to 2–2½ minutes in a higher-wattage cooker). In other words, reduce the cooking time by about one quarter.

Or better

* simply lower the microwave power level to the equivalent of 600–700W and cook for the stated time. In my experience, the MEDIUM-HIGH/70–75% setting is often the most appropriate one to use but, if in doubt, check with your instruction book or with the microwave manufacturer.

Remember, these are only guidelines – cooking times will usually vary slightly from microwave to microwave, and with the type of food and its temperature, shape and size. The first time you try a recipe/dish, underestimate the time – after all, it can always be returned to the microwave for extra cooking.

Adjusting The Cooking Times To Suit The Number Of Portions

All the recipes in this book have been developed for one person. It is a simple matter to double up on quantities if you are cooking for two. In some cases it will be more practical to cook one item at a time. If you decide to put twice the quantity (or two items) into the microwave at one time, the general rule is to add half the cooking time.

Here are extra *general* guides to adjusting the cooking times of recipes which feed 2, 4 or 6 people. They may look complicated at first, but once you get used to the idea it is quite easy.

General guide to reduce cooking times:
If a recipe states that 2 items/portions take 6 mins., divide by 3 (i.e. one extra portion). This gives you 2. Double this number to give you the cooking time for one item/portion (4 mins.). Add half this time (2 mins.) for each extra item/portion.

If a recipe states that 4 items/portions take 15 mins., divide by 5 (i.e. one extra portion). This gives you 3. Double this number to give you the cooking time for one item/portion (6 mins.). Add half the time (3 mins.) for each extra portion.

If a recipe states that 6 items/portions take 28 mins., divide by 7. This gives you 4. Double it to give the time for one portion/item (8 mins.). Add 4 mins. for each extra item/portion.

General guide to increase cooking times:
If a recipe serves one portion, add about half the cooking time for each extra portion.

When using these guidelines, all timings are approximate. They will rarely work out as conveniently as the examples above. Remember it is better to underestimate the cooking time rather than to overcook. Items like rice, pasta and dried vegetables (i.e. those foods that always need to absorb the same proportion of water) will take a similar time to cook no matter what the quantity. Use the ingredient with the longest cooking time as a guide too.

Variable Powers
Most of the recipes are cooked on HIGH/100% power. Some recipes are better cooked on DEFROST/30%, MEDIUM/50% or MEDIUM-HIGH/70–75%. Check with your instruction book to see which setting coincides with these.

In high-power microwave cookers (800–1000W) small quantities of food often benefit from being cooked or reheated on MEDIUM-HIGH/70–75% or lower.

Symbols
Alongside the majority of recipes you will find the following information:
    S: suitable for a snack
    L: suitable for lunch or supper
    M: suitable for a main meal
    Easy: the recipe is simple to prepare
    Needs a little extra care: the method may be a little long or detailed.

Standing Times

Microwave cooking generates heat within the food. This heat will not disappear simply because the microwaves are switched off at the end of the cooking period. The food will go on cooking after it comes out of the oven (just as it would from a conventional oven) and the standing times suggested in the recipes allow for this and for the temperature in the food to even out. Do not make the mistake of missing out on this standing time if you want to achieve the best results.

Ingredients

Please keep to either metric or imperial measurements. All ingredients in this book were used at room temperature. All spoon measures are level.

Drinks and Other Liquids

To prevent hot drinks and other liquids from bubbling over unexpectedly, either in the microwave or after they have been taken out of the oven, follow these guidelines.

*   use a large container to allow the liquid to bubble up.

*   avoid using cups or mugs with straight sides – those with sloping sides (where the top is wider than the bottom) are better.

*   stir liquids, drinks and sauces before, during and after microwaving.

*   do not overheat.

*   always allow a standing time so that the heat in the liquid can settle down and even out.

REMEMBER

These recipes have been developed in 600–700W micro-wave cookers.

If your microwave has a **lower wattage**, use the power levels given in the recipes and slightly increase the cooking times (see page 28).

If your microwave has a **higher wattage**, best results are often obtained if you simply lower the power level and cook for the times given in the recipes. So if a recipe cooks on:

HIGH /100%	**use**	**MEDIUM-HIGH/70–75%**
MEDIUM-HIGH/75%	**use**	**MEDIUM/50%**
MEDIUM/50%	**use**	**MEDIUM-LOW/30%**
MEDIUM-LOW/30%	**use**	**LOW/10–20%**

7

BREAKFASTS

A nutritious breakfast, it has been proved, provides stamina and 'brain power' to last several hours. The microwave will make you a hot breakfast in minutes. Here are some ideas – check the eggs section too on pages 99–105.

Fresh Coffee
Here is a useful tip if you enjoy coffee prepared by the filter or percolator methods. Instead of keeping it warm in the normal ways – for hours on a low heat – reheat individual cups or mugs in the microwave. One large cup or mug takes 1½–2 minutes on HIGH. Stir it before and during heating and do not allow it to boil. (Please read 'Drinks' on page 31.)

Instant Coffee
To make it in the microwave: stir instant coffee powder or granules into a large cup or mug of water and stir well.

Cook on HIGH for 1½–2 minutes until almost boiling, stirring once or twice. (Please read 'Drinks' on page 31.)

Tea

Heat a large cup or mug of water on HIGH for 1½–2 minutes until almost boiling, stirring once or twice. Gently drop a tea bag into the water and allow it to stand until the required strength is reached. (Please read 'Drinks' on page 31.)

Milk

Use the microwave to heat milk for drinks or for cereals. 150ml (¼ pt) takes 1–1½ minutes on HIGH. (Please read 'Drinks' on page 31.)

Croissants

Take care not to overheat croissants – they spoil easily. Sit the croissant(s) on a sheet of kitchen paper

1 croissant takes about 20 seonds on DEFROST/30%.
2 croissants take about 30 seconds on DEFROST/30%.

Hot Bread Roll

Heat a bread roll for breakfast (or refresh a stale one) on MEDIUM/50% for 20–30 seconds. It will taste freshly baked. Remember that if you heat more than one roll, add half the time per roll.

Poached Egg

Method

Best results are obtained if the egg is at room temperature.
1. Microwave 150ml (¼ pt) water with a dash of vinegar in a small container on HIGH for 1 minute or until it boils.
2. Break an egg into the water and prick its yolk.
3. Cover and microwave on HIGH for 45 seconds then allow the egg to stand (and set) for 1–2 minutes before serving on toast or grilled muffins or waffles.

Porridge

Easy
Total cooking time: 3–4 mins.

For a change add 15ml (1 tbsp) sultanas at stage 1.

Ingredients
50g (2 oz) porridge oats
150ml (¼ pt) water (check with packet instructions)
 or milk and water
sugar, honey, dried fruit or salt

Method
1. Mix together the porridge oats and cold water in a deep bowl.
2. Cook uncovered on HIGH for 3–4 minutes, stirring occasionally, until it boils.
3. When it boils, turn the power off and allow the porridge to stand for about 3 minutes before serving with sugar, honey, dried fruit or salt.

Ham and Egg in Wholemeal Roll

S/L Easy
Total cooking time: about 1 min.

This makes a suitable snack at any time of the day. For breakfast, you may prefer to leave out the cheese.

Ingredients
1 egg, size 2 or 3, beaten
15ml (1 tbsp) milk
salt and pepper
knob of butter or margarine
1 ham slice, chopped
1 wholemeal bap
1 cheese slice

Method
1. Mix together the egg, milk and seasoning in a small bowl and add the butter.
2. Cook the egg mixture on HIGH for 20 seconds and mix well with a fork.
3. Repeat stage 2 until the egg is almost set. Stir in the ham and let it stand, covered.
4. Slice the wholemeal bap and lay the cheese on the bottom half. Microwave the two halves on HIGH for 15–20 seconds.
5. Spoon the egg on to the cheese and replace the top half of the bap.

Prune and Grapefruit Compote   *Easy*
Total cooking time: 5 mins.

With the microwave there is no need to soak large dried fruit before cooking. Prepare this recipe the night before and chill it. Serve it on its own, with yoghurt or topped with muesli.

Ingredients
50g (2 oz) ready-to-eat dried prunes
150ml (¼ pt) apple juice
1 small grapefruit, peeled and segmented
sugar (optional)

Method
1. Cook the prunes and apple juice in a covered container on HIGH for 5 minutes. Cover and allow to cool.
2. Mix the grapefruit segments with the prunes in their juice.
3. Stir in sugar to taste (optional).

Smoky Kedgeree *S/L Easy*
Total cooking time: about 16 mins.

This may be prepared the evening before and simply reheated in the morning. Replace the mackerel fillets with smoked cod or haddock if you prefer.

Ingredients
80g (3 oz) long grain brown rice
5ml (1 tsp) vegetable oil
300ml (½ pt) water, boiling
grated rind and juice of half a lemon
75g (3 oz) frozen smoked mackerel fillets, thawed on DEFROST/30% for 2–3 minutes (and stand for 5 minutes)
5 ml (1 tsp) capers
30ml (2 tbsp) parsley, chopped
1 egg, hard-boiled or poached (see page 34)

Method
1. Place the rice and vegetable oil in a large bowl. Stir well and pour the boiling water over.
2. Stir in the lemon juice and rind and cook on HIGH for about 15 minutes.
3. Allow the rice to stand covered for 5 minutes to finish cooking (and to absorb any water left in the container) before using. Drain if necessary.
4. Cook the mackerel fillets in a covered container on MEDIUM/50% for 1 minute.
5. Flake the fish, removing any skin and bones and mix it into the rice with the remaining ingredients.

8

SOUPS, STARTERS & SAUCES

Fresh, dried or canned soups can be prepared in the microwave. For soups and sauces always use a container large enough to allow the liquid to boil up, particularly where milk is an ingredient. Stir soups and sauces a few times during cooking.

Lean Meat Pâté   *S/L/M Easy*
                              Total cooking time: about 15 mins.

A tasty starter, snack or lunch that is quick and simple to prepare.

Ingredients
2 rashers of streaky bacon, rindless
175g (3 oz) chicken breast, boneless
100g (4 oz) pork steak, boneless

pinch of dried thyme
pinch of ground nutmeg
salt and ground black pepper
15ml (1 tbsp) single cream or yoghurt
7.5–15ml (½–1 tbsp) brandy
1 small egg, beaten

Method
1. Stretch the bacon rashers with the back of a knife. Cut them and use them to line a small basin.
2. Chop the meats roughly before mixing with the remaining ingredients.
3. Pour the mixture into the bacon-lined basin, pack down tightly and cover.
4. Cook on MEDIUM/50% for 14–15 minutes.
5. Drain off the liquid, cover with foil, place a weight on top and allow the pâté to cool before chilling and serving.

Sweetcorn Mousse   *S/L/M Needs a little extra care*
                        Total cooking time: about 10 mins.

A delicately-flavoured mousse using a white sauce as a base. You will need a food processor or blender for this recipe.

Ingredients
100g (4 oz) sweetcorn kernels, thawed on DEFROST/30% for about 2 minutes (and stand for 5 minutes) or drained canned
3 spring onions, chopped
15g (½ oz) butter or margarine
15g (½ oz) plain flour
75ml (3 fl oz) milk
15ml (1 tbsp) fresh white breadcrumbs
1 small egg, beaten   *(continued overleaf)*

(Sweetcorn Mousse continued)
pinch of cayenne pepper
salt and ground black pepper
chives, chopped, to garnish

Method
1. Place the sweetcorn and onions in a bowl, cover and cook on HIGH for 3 minutes.
2. Whisk the butter, flour and milk together in a separate bowl. Microwave on HIGH for 2–3 minutes until the sauce thickens and boils, whisking frequently during cooking.
3. Stir the breadcrumbs into the sauce.
4. Blend the sweetcorn and onion for a few seconds (using a food processor or blender) and beat the mixture into the sauce with the egg, cayenne and seasoning.
5. Pour the mousse into a suitable bowl and cook uncovered on MEDIUM/50% for about 5 minutes or until just set.
6. Allow the mousse to stand for 10 minutes before turning out and garnishing with chopped chives. Serve with crispy bread, toast or biscuits.

Sweetcorn and Crispy Bacon Soup   *S/L/M Easy*
                                Total cooking time: 4–6 mins.

If cooking this soup in advance, add the bacon at the last minute only.

Ingredients
1 rasher of streaky bacon
3 spring onions, chopped
1 small bay leaf
150ml (¼ pt) chicken stock
75g (3 oz) canned sweetcorn, drained
5–10ml (1–2 tsp) cornflour

45ml (3 tbsp) milk
salt and ground black pepper

Method
1. Place the bacon rasher on a small rack on a plate. Cook on HIGH for 1 minute or until the bacon is crisp.
2. Put the spring onions, bay leaf, chicken stock and sweetcorn into a bowl, cover and cook on HIGH for 2 minutes, stirring once during cooking.
3. Blend the cornflour with the milk and stir it into the sweetcorn mixture.
4. Cover and cook on HIGH for 1–2 minutes.
5. Season to taste, remove the bay leaf, chop the crispy bacon and sprinkle over the dish before serving.

Quick Pea Soup

S/L/M Easy
Total cooking time: 5–6 mins.

Serve this soup with a good sprinkling of freshly ground black pepper.

Ingredients
4 spring onions, chopped
knob of butter or margarine
50g (2 oz) potato, grated or chopped finely
2.5ml (½ tsp) mint sauce, ready-made
50g (2 oz) frozen peas
150ml (¼ pt) chicken stock, hot
salt and ground black pepper
15–30ml (1–2 tbsp) milk

Method
1. Place the onions, butter and potato in a bowl, cover and cook on HIGH for 2 minutes.
2. Stir in the mint sauce, frozen peas, hot chicken stock and seasoning. Cover and cook on HIGH for 3 minutes.

3. Sieve, liquidise or purée the soup, then stir in the milk.
4. Reheat the soup on HIGH for 1 minute before serving.

Bacon and Olive Kebabs   *S/L/M Easy*
Total cooking time: about 2 mins.

Use stuffed green olives and omit the red pepper if preferred.

Ingredients
2 rashers of streaky bacon
4 black olives
1cm (½ in) slice of red pepper, cut into small squares

Method
1. Cut each bacon rasher into three and fold them loosely. Thread the bacon, olives and red pepper alternately on to two small wooden skewers.
2. Place the kebabs on a microwave rack on a plate.
3. Cook on HIGH for about 2 minutes or until the bacon is cooked.

Stock Pot   *Easy*
Total cooking time: about 13 mins.

The flavour of this speedy stock is better if cold water is used and brought up to the boil in the microwave rather than adding boiling water to the ingredients. Washed peelings (of root vegetables such as carrots, parsnips, swede etc.) can be used too. Use the stock in sauces, gravies, soups such as Lentil Soup (page 44) and casseroles – Vegetable Casserole (page 90).

Ingredients
1 small onion, sliced
1 carrot, sliced
1 stick of celery, chopped
2–3 mushrooms, halved
300ml (½ pt) water
1 bay leaf
few sprigs of parsley
6 black peppercorns
salt

Method
1. Place all the ingredients with a little salt in a deep container, cover and bring to the boil on HIGH (about 3 minutes).
2. Once the mixture is boiling, cover and cook on MEDIUM-HIGH/75% for 10 minutes.
3. Remove the vegetables, and the stock is ready for use. Save the vegetables to serve in a white or cheese sauce (see page 48) browned under the grill. Alternatively, purée them and use as a sauce with meat or fish.

French Onion Soup with Herb Croûtons

L/M Easy
Total cooking time: about 10 mins.

This makes a filling dish. The croûtons are best used on the day they are made.

Ingredients
5ml (1 tsp) vegetable oil
small knob of butter
225g (8 oz) onions, thinly sliced
5ml (1 tsp) dark brown sugar
½–1 garlic clove, crushed
150ml (¼ pt) water

(continued overleaf)

(French Onion Soup with Herb Croûtons continued)
15ml (1 tbsp) mushroom ketchup
2.5ml (½ tsp) Worcestershire sauce
salt and ground black pepper
1 slice of bread
butter
1.25ml (¼ tsp) mixed dried herbs

Method
1. Place the vegetable oil, butter, onions and brown sugar into a deep container, cover and cook on HIGH for 3 minutes.
2. Stir well and cook on HIGH for 1 minute.
3. Add the garlic, water, mushroom ketchup, Worcestershire sauce and seasoning to taste. Cover, cook on HIGH for 5 minutes, stirring halfway through cooking, then allow the soup to stand covered for 5 minutes.
4. To prepare the croûtons, thinly spread the bread slice with butter and sprinkle the herbs over the butter.
5. Cut the bread into small cubes and spread them over a large heatproof plate.
6. Microwave the bread cubes on HIGH for 1–1½ minutes until they begin to crispen. Rearrange them once or twice during cooking. They will continue crispening as they cool.
7. Reheat the soup on HIGH for 1 minute if necessary, adding extra water if it is too thick.
8. Sprinkle the croûtons over the soup, then serve.

Lentil Soup   *L/M Easy*
                    Total cooking time: 25–30 mins.

Soups made with dried lentils are no longer a chore to make for one person. The microwave eliminates sticky, burnt pans and the necessity for continuous checking and topping up with liquid during cooking.

Ingredients
4 spring onions, chopped
1 carrot, finely chopped
1 rasher of bacon, chopped
300ml (½ pt) water or stock (see page 42)
pinch of ground cumin
25g (1 oz) lentils
salt and ground black pepper
5ml (1 tsp) lemon juice

Method
1. Place the onions, carrot and bacon into a deep container, cover and cook on HIGH for 2 minutes.
2. Add the remaining ingredients, stir well and bring to the boil on HIGH (about 3–3½ minutes).
3. Cover and cook on MEDIUM/50% for 20–30 minutes or until the lentils are tender.
4. Liquidise or blend the soup adding extra liquid if required and adjust the seasoning if necessary.

Thick Vegetable Soup

L/M Easy
Total cooking time: about 20 mins.

This is a good recipe for using up odds and ends from the store cupboard or salad drawer of the fridge. The cooking time can be cut down by microwaving on HIGH throughout.

Ingredients
15g (½ oz) butter or margarine
1 small onion, chopped
1 small potato, chopped
½ small parsnip, chopped
1 small carrot, chopped
7.5ml (½ tbsp) chopped parsley
pinch of mixed dried herbs
pinch of ground nutmeg *(continued overleaf)*

(Thick Vegetable Soup continued)
300ml (½ pt) vegetable stock (see Stock Pot, page 42)
15g (½ oz) lettuce (outer leaves), shredded
salt and ground black pepper

Method
1. Put the butter, onion, potato, parsnip, and carrot in a deep container, cover and cook on HIGH for 4 minutes.
2. Add the parsley, herbs, nutmeg to taste and the vegetable stock and bring to the boil on HIGH (about 3–3½ minutes).
3. Cover and cook on MEDIUM-HIGH/75% for 10 minutes (or on HIGH for 7–8 minutes) or until the vegetables are tender, stirring halfway through cooking.
4. Blend or liquidise the soup at this stage if liked.
5. Stir in the lettuce and seasoning to taste, cover and cook on HIGH for 3 minutes.

Courgette and Carrot Soup with Tagliatelli

L/M Easy
Total cooking time: 13 mins.

A small amount of pasta (or use rice if you like) makes this a filling soup.

Ingredients
1 medium courgette, finely chopped
1 carrot, finely chopped
1 stick of celery, finely chopped
1 garlic clove, crushed
15g (½ oz) butter or margarine
300ml (½ pt) stock or water
15ml (1 tbsp) tomato purée
1.25ml (¼ tsp) dried basil
salt and ground black pepper
15g (½ oz) tagliatelli, broken up

30–45ml (2–3 tbsp) milk
5ml (1 tsp) chopped parsley

Method
1. Place the first five ingredients in a deep container, cover and cook on HIGH for 3 minutes.
2. Add the stock or water, tomato purée, basil, seasoning and tagliatelli, cover and cook on HIGH for 10 minutes.
3. Stir in the milk and parsley and allow the soup to stand for 3 minutes before serving.

'Crostini' Bread Roll   *S/L/M Easy*
Total cooking time: about 1½ mins.

This makes quite a substantial snack or starter. Take care not to overheat the roll or the crust will become rubbery.

Ingredients
15g (½ oz) butter
½ garlic clove, crushed
ground black pepper
1 bread roll
2 cheese slices, thin
2 ham slices, thin

Method
1. Soften the butter if necessary in a small bowl on DEFROST/30% for a few seconds.
2. Mix the garlic with the butter, adding black pepper to taste.
3. Cut the bread roll in two places, without taking the knife through the bottom crust. Spread half the butter in each slit.
4. Place a slice of cheese and ham in each slit and press the roll together again.
5. Wrap the roll in greaseproof paper and cook on

DEFROST/30% for 1–1½ minutes or until the cheese just melts.

White Sauce

S/L/M Easy
Total cooking time: about 3½ mins.

Small quantities of sauces are simple to prepare in the microwave. Use a small bowl or jug.

Ingredients
15g (½ oz) butter
15g (½ oz) flour
150ml (¼ pt) milk
salt and pepper

Method
1. Cook the butter on HIGH for about 30 seconds until melted.
2. Stir in the flour then gradually add the milk, stirring well.
3. Cook on HIGH for 2–3 minutes, stirring every 30 seconds, until the sauce thickens, boils and rises up the container.

Cheese Sauce: Add a pinch of dry mustard at stage 2, and 25–50g (1–2 oz) grated cheese after stage 3. Allow the sauce to stand so that the cheese just melts into it.

Mushroom Sauce: Add 25g (1oz) finely sliced mushrooms after stage 1 and cook, with the butter, on HIGH for 30 seconds before continuing with stage 2.

Onion Sauce: Add ½ small chopped onion or 2–3 chopped spring onions after stage 1. Cook the onions and butter on HIGH for about 1 minute before continuing with stage 2.

Parsley Sauce: Add 10ml (2 tsp) chopped parsley after stage 3.

Prawn Sauce: Add 25–40g (1–1½ oz) peeled prawns and a little tomato purée after stage 3.

Poppadums

Brush one side of a poppadum with cooking oil and place it on a sheet of non-stick or greaseproof paper. Cook on HIGH for ½–1 minute until crisp. Two poppadums cook more evenly than one and take 1–1½ minutes (turn them round halfway through cooking).

Alternatively, omit the oil and cook poppadums as above.

9

FISH

If you have used a microwave before you will know that it cooks fish beautifully. If you have yet to try it, then do so as soon as possible!

CHECKPOINTS FOR FISH
* Cover fish to keep in the juices. Microwave (or roasting) bags and boil-in-the-bags are useful for this – tuck the open ends under the fish so that steam can escape.

* Fish needs no liquid when cooking it in the microwave. If you intend to make a sauce, cook the fish in just sufficient liquid for this purpose.

* A whole fish cooks more evenly if the head and tail are wrapped in small pieces of smooth foil. Check with your instruction book regarding the use of foil. Make a

slit in the skin each side of the fish to prevent it breaking open. When cooking two or more whole fish, arrange them head to tail (no need to use foil), and side by side, to encourage even cooking.

*   Salt after cooking or the surface of the fish will dry out.

*   When cooking with butter, melt it and brush it over the fish to encourage even cooking.

*   Fish is cooked when the flakes separate easily. If the flesh inside is still slightly translucent, simply lay the flakes together again, cover the fish and allow it to stand for a few minutes. By this stage it should be cooked to perfection.

All the instructions in these recipes assume the fish has been gutted or prepared.

Guide to cooking times			
Piece	*Weight*	*Minutes on HIGH*	*Standing time (mins.)*
Whole fish e.g. trout or mackerel	175g (6 oz)	2–3	3–5
Fillet: thick thin	175g (6 oz) 100–150g (4–5 oz)	2–3 1½–2	3–5 3–5
If you find that fish cooked on HIGH *tends to spit and overcook, try reducing the power to* MEDIUM *and cooking for a little longer.*			

Cod and Lime Kebabs
L/M Easy
Total cooking time: about 2 mins.

Replace the lime with lemon if liked. Delicious as a starter or a light lunch with brown rice and salad.

Ingredients
50g (2 oz) cod portion, cut into 6 cubes
2 lime slices, halved
15g (½ oz) butter
2.5ml (½ tsp) dried tarragon
salt and freshly ground black pepper

Method
1.   Thread the cod cubes and lime slices alternately on to two small wooden skewers.
2.   In a small container, cook the butter on HIGH for 15–30 seconds until melted. Brush the butter over the fish and lime.
3.   Sprinkle the kebabs with the dried tarragon and place them on a microwave rack on a plate.
4.   Cook uncovered on HIGH for 1–1½ minutes.
5.   Sprinkle with salt and freshly ground black pepper and serve.

Salmon with Cucumber Sauce
L/M Easy
Total cooking time: about 6 mins.

This is a deliciously light dish – ideal for a warm summer day. Best results are obtained if the salmon and sauce are cooked separately.

Ingredients
knob of butter
40g (1½ oz) cucumber, skin left on, cut into small strips
2.5ml (½ tsp) dried tarragon
**   OR 5ml (1 tsp) fresh tarragon**

salt and ground black pepper
175g (6 oz) salmon steak
1 spring onion, chopped
5ml (1 tsp) cornflour
5ml (1 tsp) white wine vinegar or lemon juice
15ml (1 tbsp) cream or plain yoghurt

Method
1. In a small jug melt the butter on HIGH for 20–30 seconds and stir in the cucumber, tarragon and seasoning.
2. Cover and cook on HIGH for 1 minute.
3. Place the salmon in a shallow container and sprinkle with the spring onion. Cover and cook on HIGH for 2 minutes. Test the salmon by inserting a fork between the flakes. The flakes of the fish should separate quite easily. If the fish is slightly translucent in the centre, simply lay the flakes back in place, cover and allow the fish to stand for a few minutes before continuing with stage 4.
4. Pour the fish juices into the cucumber and tarragon mixture then stir in the cornflour followed by the vinegar or lemon juice.
5. Cook the sauce on HIGH, stirring every 30 seconds until it thickens and boils.
6. Stir the cream or yoghurt into the sauce, pour it over the salmon and serve.

Fish with a Spanish Flavour
L/M Easy
Total cooking time: 6–8 mins.

Make the sauce first, then you can cook the fish to perfection before coating it.

Ingredients
3 spring onions, chopped

(continued overleaf)

(Fish with a Spanish Flavour continued)
5ml (1 tsp) olive oil (optional)
½ green (or red) pepper, chopped
1 garlic clove, crushed
30ml (2 tbsp) tomato purée
75ml (5 tbsp) white wine or dry cider
salt and ground black pepper
3 black olives, chopped
175g (6 oz) cod, haddock or hake fillet
10ml (2 tsp) lemon juice

Method
1. Cook the onions, olive oil (optional) and pepper on HIGH in a covered container for 2 minutes.
2. Stir in the garlic, tomato purée, wine or cider, and seasoning. Cover and cook on HIGH for 2–3 minutes, stirring twice during cooking.
3. Add the black olives, cover and allow the sauce to stand while the fish cooks.
4. Place the fish in a shallow container and sprinkle with the lemon juice and some black pepper.
5. Cover and cook on HIGH for 2 minutes. Test the fish as in stage 3 of Salmon with Cucumber Sauce on page 53.
6. Pour the sauce over the fish, reheat on HIGH if necessary for ½–1 minute and serve.

Smoked Haddock 'Crumble'   *S/L/M Easy*
                        Total cooking time: about 7 mins.

The bran flakes make the topping light, healthy and different.

Ingredients
**200g (7 oz) 'Boil-in-the-bag' smoked cod or haddock with
    butter, frozen**
5ml (1 tsp) chopped parsley

1 small gherkin, chopped
5ml (1 tsp) lemon or lime juice
30ml (2 tbsp) cream or yoghurt
salt and ground black pepper
15g (½ oz) bran flakes

Method
1. Place the frozen 'boil-in-the-bag' fish in a small shallow container. Slit the bag and cook on HIGH for 4–5 minutes.
2. Allow the fish to stand for 2 minutes before cutting the bag and turning the fish and butter out into the shallow container. Discard the bag, any dividing paper and bones, and flake the fish.
3. Stir in the remaining ingredients except the bran flakes, cover and cook on HIGH for 30 seconds.
4. Sprinkle the bran flakes over the fish mixture and cook on HIGH for 30 seconds. Serve immediately.

Trout with Butter and Mustard Sauce

L/M Easy
Total cooking time: about 6½ mins.

Mustard complements the texture and flavour of trout beautifully.

Ingredients
175g (6 oz) trout
25g (1 oz) butter
5ml (1 tsp) wine vinegar
5ml (1 tsp) whole grain mustard
black pepper
parsley to garnish

Method
1. Wash and dry the cavity of the fish. Slit the skin in two or three places to prevent it splitting open during cooking.

2.   Place the trout in a shallow container, cover and cook on MEDIUM/50% for 4–5 minutes (cover the head and tail with small areas of foil to prevent them overcooking – check with your manufacturer's instructions concerning the use of foil).
3.   Drain and save the juices. Place the fish on a warm serving dish, cover and allow it to stand while you prepare the sauce.
4.   Cook the butter with the fish juices on HIGH for 30 seconds.
5.   Stir in the remaining ingredients, except the parsley, and cook on HIGH for 1 minute.
6.   Pour the sauce over the trout and serve garnished with parsley.

Prawns in Tomato Sauce   *L/M Easy*
Total cooking time: about 7½ mins.

This quick and tasty treat will become a favourite. Delicious on a bed of rice or pasta ribbons.

Ingredients
1 small onion, chopped
1 garlic clove, crushed
15ml (1 tbsp) chopped green pepper
200g can of tomatoes, chopped
2 drops Tabasco
salt and ground black pepper
100g (4 oz) peeled prawns, thawed on DEFROST/30% for 2–
    2½ minutes (and stand for 3 minutes)
10ml (2 tsp) lemon juice

Method
1.   Place the onion, garlic and green pepper in a container, cover and cook on HIGH for 2 minutes.
2.   Stir in the tomatoes, tabasco and seasoning, cover and cook for 5 minutes.

3. Add the prawns and lemon juice. Cook uncovered on HIGH for 30 seconds.
4. Stir well, adjusting the seasoning, before serving.

Tuna Stir-Fry   *L/M Easy*
Total cooking time: 7–8 mins.

This dish has more flavour if it is cooked in a browning dish. Don't miss out if you do not have one though!

Ingredients
10ml (2 tsp) vegetable oil
1 small onion, chopped
1 garlic clove, crushed
2 celery sticks, chopped
½ green pepper, chopped
50g (2 oz) button mushrooms, sliced
15ml (1 tbsp) frozen sweetcorn
salt and ground black pepper
184g can of tuna fish, drained and flaked
15ml (1 tbsp) lemon juice
chopped parsley, to taste

Method
1. Preheat a browning dish on HIGH for 5 minutes, add the oil and stir in the onion, garlic and celery. Cover and cook on HIGH for 5 minutes, stirring once during cooking.

or

Place the oil, onion, garlic and celery in a container, cover and cook on HIGH for 6 minutes, stirring once during cooking.

2. Allow it to stand covered for a few minutes before adding the pepper, mushrooms and sweetcorn. Cover and cook on HIGH for 1 minute.
3. Season to taste and stir in the tuna flakes, lemon juice and parsley to taste.
4. Cover and cook on HIGH for 1 minute.

Buttered Plaice with Capers   *L/M Easy*
Total cooking time: 3–4 mins.

The capers could be replaced with 5ml (1 tsp) chopped fresh herbs for a simple but delicious flavour.

Ingredients
25g (1 oz) butter
15–25g (½–1 oz) capers, drained
5ml (1 tsp) parsley, chopped
ground black pepper
1 large plaice fillet
5ml (1 tsp) lemon juice

Method
1. In a small container, cook the butter for 30–45 seconds until melted.
2. Stir in the capers, parsley and black pepper to taste. Cover and cook for 30 seconds on HIGH.
3. Brush a little of the melted butter over the base of a shallow container and lay the plaice in it.
4. Brush over sufficient of the butter mixture just to coat the fish. Cover and cook on HIGH for 1–1½ minutes.
5. Reheat the rest of the butter mix on HIGH for 20–30 seconds and pour it over the plaice. Sprinkle over the lemon juice and allow the dish to stand, covered for 2–3 minutes.

Kippers with Tartare Sauce *S/L/M Easy*
Total cooking time: about 3½ mins.

This unusual flavour mix is very successful. Try serving this with scrambled egg and/or wholemeal bread.

Ingredients
200g (7 oz) 'Boil-in-the-bag' kippers, thawed on DEFROST/
30% (pierce the bag) for 4–5 minutes (and stand for 5
minutes)
10ml (2 tsp) tartare sauce
ground black pepper

Method
1. Split the bag and place it in a shallow container.
2. Through the split, spread the tartare sauce over the kippers.
3. Cook on HIGH for 3½ minutes.
4. Allow the kippers to stand for 2–3 minutes before turning them out of the bag and sprinkling with black pepper to taste.

Sweet and Sour Prawns *L/M Easy*
Total cooking time: 12–13 mins.

This will serve two as a starter. If you cannot get fresh beansprouts, simply reheat a can of drained beansprouts in a covered container on HIGH for 1–2 minutes at stage 3.

Ingredients
10ml (2 tsp) cornflour
30ml (2 tbsp) water
45ml (3 tbsp) tomato ketchup
10ml (2 tsp) chilli sauce
1 garlic clove, crushed

(continued overleaf)

(Sweet and Sour Prawns continued)
**225g (8 oz) prawns, thawed on DEFROST/30% for 3–4
    minutes (and stand for 5 minutes)**
5ml (1 tsp) lemon juice
225g (8 oz) beansprouts
15ml (1 tbsp) soy sauce

Method
1. In a deep bowl or container mix together the
    cornflour and water, then stir in the tomato ketchup,
    chilli sauce and garlic. Cook on HIGH for 2–3 minutes,
    stirring frequently until the mixture has thickened.
2. Stir in the prawns, cover and cook on MEDIUM-HIGH/
    75% for 7 minutes, stirring once during cooking. Stir
    in the lemon juice and allow to stand while the
    beansprouts are prepared.
3. Place the beansprouts in a large container with 30ml
    (2 tbsp) water. Cover and cook on HIGH for about 3
    minutes or until tender, shaking or stirring them
    halfway through cooking.
4. Drain the beansprouts and toss them in the soy sauce.
5. Spoon the prawns and their sauce over the bean-
    sprouts.

Moules Marinière
L/M Easy
Total cooking time: about 5 mins.

Mussels are perfect for microwaving. Discard any which
have not opened during cooking.

Ingredients
15g (½ oz) butter
3 spring onions, chopped
**0.5 litre (1 pt) fresh mussels, soaked in several changes of
    water for at least 8 hours or overnight, scrubbed and
    beards scraped away**

ground black pepper
30–45ml (2–3 tbsp) dry white wine
30ml (2 tbsp) double cream
chopped parsley to garnish

Method
1. In a large container, cook the butter on HIGH for 30 seconds until melted.
2. Stir the onions into the butter, cover and cook on HIGH for 1 minute.
3. Add the mussels, pepper and wine, cover and cook on HIGH for 2½–3 minutes, shaking once or twice during cooking, until all the mussel shells have opened.
4. Use a slotted spoon to lift the mussels out of the juice and into a warmed serving dish.
5. Stir the cream into the mussel juices and cook on HIGH for 30 seconds.
6. Pour the sauce over the mussels and sprinkle with plenty of chopped parsley.

Fish en Papillotte

L/M Easy
Total cooking time: about 5 mins.

Cooking in a paper parcel is an ideal method for a fish fillet or steak. Serve it in its cooking paper and enjoy the delicious aroma as you open the parcel.

Ingredients
15ml (1 tbsp) chopped fresh herbs such as parsley or dill
25g (1 oz) butter
1 small carrot, shredded
1 small celery stick, chopped
2 spring onions, chopped
175g (6 oz) fish steak or fillet, such as cod or salmon

Method
1. Beat the herbs into the butter.
2. Cook the carrot, celery and onions in a small covered bowl on HIGH for 2 minutes.
3. Place the fish on a square of non-stick or greaseproof paper, large enough to enclose the fish completely.
4. Drain the vegetables and spoon them over the fish. Top with the herb butter.
5. Fold the paper over the fish and tuck the open ends underneath. Place in a shallow dish.
6. Cook on HIGH for 2–3 minutes. Allow to stand for 2–3 minutes before serving.

10

MEAT & POULTRY

The advantages of cooking small portions of meat in the microwave include speed, flavour retention and less shrinkage – particularly when the power level is turned down. Add to this the lack of messy frying pans and/or saucepans and you have some very good reasons for using the microwave to cook meat.

The only drawback is that small portions will not brown in the microwave. There are ways to overcome this – for instance, by browning or finishing off under your grill (or the browning element in the microwave, if you have one). You will no doubt have also seen microwave browning powders on the market. In general these are very good but use them with caution for the first time as they tend to be highly flavoured. A browning dish is useful for cooking meat – you can sear the outside of the meat first and then finish cooking by microwave. A delicious method of browning meat and poultry in the microwave is to brush it with equal quantities of mustard, Worcestershire sauce and cooking oil before cooking. Alternatively you may prefer to cook meat (chops, sausages, burgers and steaks in particular) under the conventional grill while you prepare the accompanying vegetables and/or sauce in the microwave.

CHECKPOINTS FOR MEAT & POULTRY

* Even-shaped pieces cook best in the microwave. Help uneven pieces (like a chicken leg) to cook more evenly by wrapping the thin end with a small piece of smooth foil. (Check with your manufacturer's instructions regarding the use of foil.) Alternatively, using a lower power level (such as MEDIUM/50%) also encourages even cooking.

* Minced meat should be stirred several times during cooking to break up the pieces.

* Cover meat and poultry during cooking, if only to save the oven walls from splashes.

* Salt pieces of meat after cooking or it will dry and toughen the surface.

* When necessary, secure meat or poultry pieces with string or wooden (not metal) skewers.

* Cook pieces of meat or poultry on a rack in a shallow container. This makes sure that they do not sit (and 'stew') in their own juices during cooking, and that the microwaves can reach the meat from every angle. Cover with kitchen paper to absorb fat and steam, and to prevent splashing on the oven walls.

* Turn over meat pieces halfway through cooking, to encourage even results.

The following chart gives suitable quantities of meat and poultry for a single portion, with the appropriate cooking and standing times. Times are given for cooking on HIGH.

Guide to cooking times			
Piece	*Weight*	*Minutes on HIGH*	*Standing time (mins.)*
Bacon rashers:	2 back	2–2½	1–2
	2 middle	3	1–2
	2 streaky	2	1–2
Beefburgers:			
frozen	2 × 50g (2 oz)	3–4	2–3
fresh	2 × 100g (4 oz)	5	3–5
Chicken:			
drumsticks	2	4–6	4–5
joint	175–200g (6–7 oz)	4–5	4–5
Chops:			
Bacon	175g (6 oz)	3–3½	2–3
Lamb	175g (6 oz)	3½–4	3–5
Pork	175g (6 oz)	4–4½	3–5
Duck portion	Follow basic method in recipe on page 82.		
Gammon steak (snip the fat to prevent curling)	175g (6 oz)	3–3½	2–3
Liver	100g (4 oz)	2–3	2–3
Minced beef	Follow method and times in a similar recipe (see Spicy Cottage Pie, page 70, and Bolognese, page 67).		

Steaks and sausages need slightly more gentle cooking and are best done on a browning dish (follow the manufacturer's instructions).

Guide to cooking times			
Piece	*Weight*	*Minutes on* MEDIUM/ HIGH *(70–75%)*	*Standing time (mins.)*
Steak: rare medium well done	175g (6 oz) 175g (6 oz) 175g (6 oz)	1½–2½ 2½–3 3–4	3 3 3
Sausages:	2 large, pricked	2–3	3

Chicken breasts also require more gentle cooking if they are not to toughen. Place the whole chicken breast in a small container, cover and cook on MEDIUM/50% for 4–5 minutes or until the chicken is firm and the juice runs clear when pierced with a skewer. Allow the chicken to stand, covered, for 3 minutes before serving.

Braising and stewing need long slow cooking even in the microwave. However you will still reduce the cooking time dramatically. It is a good idea to cook on HIGH until very hot or boiling, then turn the power level down to MEDIUM/50% or DEFROST/30% and continue cooking until the meat is tender. Cooking times will depend on the quality of the meat, but check with a similar recipe in the following pages. Cut the meat into even-size pieces to encourage even cooking.

Bolognese Sauce   *L/M Easy*
Total cooking time: about 20 mins.

Replace the carrot with mushrooms or green pepper if liked. Serve with spaghetti – see page 106.

Ingredients
1 small onion, chopped
1 rasher of streaky bacon, rindless, chopped
1 small carrot, chopped
100g (4 oz) lean minced beef
230g can of tomatoes, chopped
1.25ml (¼ tsp) mixed dried herbs
1 small garlic clove, crushed
salt and pepper

Method
1. Place the onion, bacon and carrot in a small, deep container, cover and cook on HIGH for 2 minutes.
2. Stir in the minced beef, breaking it up with a fork. Cover and cook on HIGH for 4 minutes, stirring once during cooking.
3. Stir in the remaining ingredients, cover and cook on HIGH for 3 minutes, stirring once. Cover and continue cooking on MEDIUM/50% for about 10 minutes, stirring once or twice during cooking.

Beef Kebabs with Herbs   *L/M Easy*
Total cooking time: about 4 mins.

Always use wooden skewers when microwaving kebabs. Delicious served with lemon wedges, rice and a mixed salad.

Ingredients
100g (4 oz) lean minced beef
3–4 spring onions, finely chopped   *(continued overleaf)*

(Beef Kebabs with Herbs continued)
pinch of garlic granules
15g (½ oz) fresh breadcrumbs
10ml (2 tsp) tomato purée
salt and black pepper
7.5ml (½ tbsp) mixed dried herbs

Method
1. Mix together all the ingredients until they are combined, then divide the mixture into three portions.
2. Shape each portion into a 'sausage' around a wooden skewer, squeezing each one firmly so that it stays in place. Leave a small gap between them.
3. Put the kebab on a microwave rack on a plate and cook on HIGH for 2½–4 minutes. Turn the kebab over once or twice during cooking.

Chilli con Carne

L/M Easy
Total cooking time: about 15 mins.

This dish is speedy to make – even for one. Use a can of kidney beans. Adjust the quantity of chilli powder to suit your taste.

Ingredients
1 small onion, chopped
1 garlic clove, crushed
½ red or green pepper, chopped
100g (4 oz) lean minced beef
125g can of red kidney beans, drained
pinch of ground cumin
1.25–5ml (¼–1 tsp) chilli powder, to taste
15ml (1 tbsp) tomato purée
15ml (1 tbsp) red wine or water
salt and ground black pepper

Method
1. Cook the onion, garlic and red or green pepper in a covered container on HIGH for 2 minutes.
2. Stir in the remaining ingredients, cover and cook on HIGH for 3 minutes. Stir well.
3. Cover and cook on MEDIUM/50% for about 10 minutes, stirring once during cooking.
4. Allow the dish to stand covered for 5 minutes before stirring and serving with fresh crusty bread.

Bobouti

L/M Needs a little extra care
Total cooking time: about 12 mins.

This dish originates from South Africa.

Ingredients
15g (½ oz) brown bread
60ml (4 tbsp) milk
1 small onion, chopped
5ml (1 tsp) vegetable oil
100g (4 oz) lean minced beef
2.5–5ml (½–1 tsp) curry powder, to taste
1.25ml (¼ tsp) ground cinnamon
1.25ml (¼ tsp) turmeric
10ml (2 tsp) apricot jam
15g (½ oz) seedless raisins
5ml (1 tsp) lemon juice
1 egg, size 3
2 drops of almond flavouring
pinch of mustard powder
salt and ground black pepper
paprika to garnish

Method
1. Soak the bread in the milk for a few minutes.
2. Place the onion and vegetable oil in a container, cover and cook on HIGH for 2 minutes.

3. Stir in the minced beef, curry powder, cinnamon, turmeric, jam, raisins and lemon juice.
4. Squeeze out the bread, reserving the milk, and crumble it into the mince mix.
5. Cover and cook on HIGH for 5 minutes, stirring once or twice during cooking. Level the surface.
6. Mix the reserved milk with the egg, almond flavouring mustard powder and seasoning. Pour the mixture over the mince.
7. Cook on MEDIUM/50% for about 5 minutes or until the egg custard surface is set. Sprinkle with freshly ground black pepper or paprika and serve.

Spicy Cottage Pie

L/M Easy
Total cooking time: about 25 mins.

This method saves mashing the potato – cook it whole, slice it and layer it over the savoury mince base.

Ingredients
175g (6 oz) potato, scrubbed and pricked
1 small onion, chopped
1 small carrot, chopped
5ml (1 tsp) vegetable oil
100g (4 oz) lean minced beef
15ml (1 tbsp) tomato purée
2.5ml (½ tsp) mixed dried herbs
15ml (1 tbsp) water
5ml (1 tsp) Worcestershire sauce
5ml (1 tsp) mustard powder
salt and ground black pepper
25g (1 oz) cheese, grated (optional)

Method
1. Cook the potato on HIGH for 5–6 minutes, turning it over halfway through cooking.

2. Wrap the potato in foil and allow it to stand while you prepare the mince base.
3. Put the onion, carrot and vegetable oil into a flameproof container, cover and cook on HIGH for 2 minutes.
4. Stir in the minced beef, cover and cook on HIGH for 2 minutes.
5. Stir well, add the remaining ingredients (except the cheese), cover and cook on HIGH for 4 minutes.
6. Stir well, cover and continue cooking on MEDIUM/50% for about 10 minutes.
7. Slice the potato and arrange the layers on top of the mince base.
8. Sprinkle with cheese and brown the surface under a hot grill.

Cheeseburgers   *S/L Easy*
Total cooking time: 2–3 mins.

There is nothing as good as a home-made burger in a fresh bread roll. Here is a speedy version. The colour of the burgers improves while they stand. Use a browning dish if you prefer.

Ingredients
100g (4 oz) lean minced beef
½ small onion, finely chopped
25g (1 oz) bran flakes or corn flakes, crushed
25g (1 oz) mature Cheddar cheese, grated
5ml (1 tsp) Worcestershire sauce
salt and ground black pepper
15ml (1 tbsp) egg, beaten

Method
1. Mix together all the ingredients and shape into two burgers.

2.   Place the burgers on a microwave rack on a plate and cook on HIGH for 2–3 minutes, turning them over halfway through cooking.
3.   Allow the burgers to stand, covered, for 3 minutes before serving.

Honeyed Spare Ribs
L/M Easy
Total cooking time: about 16 mins.

Serve these on a bed of rice with some raw spring onions.

Ingredients
350g (12 oz) pork spare ribs
2 spring onions, chopped
15ml (1 tbsp) clear honey
5ml (1 tsp) dark soft brown sugar
few drops Worcestershire sauce
10ml (2 tsp) tomato ketchup
5ml (1 tsp) French mustard
pinch of ground ginger
pinch of mixed dried herbs
pinch of garlic powder

Method
1.   Arrange the spare ribs in one layer in a shallow dish, cover and cook on HIGH for 3 minutes. Drain and discard any fat.
2.   Mix together the remaining ingredients and pour over the ribs, coating them well.
3.   Cover and cook on HIGH for 3 minutes then spoon the juices over the ribs.
4.   Cook, uncovered, on DEFROST/30% for 5 minutes, then spoon the juices over again.
5.   Turn the power back up to HIGH and cook uncovered for 4–5 minutes, stirring halfway through cooking, or until the sauce thickens and coats the ribs well.
6.   Allow a standing time of 3–5 minutes before serving.

Pork with Apple and Walnut Stuffing   *L/M*

Needs a little extra care
Total cooking time: about 8 mins.

For a thicker sauce, remove the pork after stage 5 and keep it covered. Stir in 5ml (1 tsp) of cornflour and bring the sauce to the boil on HIGH, stirring once or twice.

Ingredients
2 spring onions, chopped
½ apple, cored and sliced
5–10ml (1–2 tsp) chopped walnuts
salt and ground black pepper
pinch of dried sage
175–225g (6–8 oz) lean pork steak
120ml (4 fl oz) dry cider

Method
1. In a small covered container cook the onions and apple on HIGH for 2 minutes. Stir in the walnuts, seasoning and sage. Allow the mixture to cool a little.
2. Place the pork between two sheets of greaseproof or non-stick paper and beat with a rolling pin until it is about 0.5cm (¼ in) thick.
3. Spread the stuffing over the pork, roll it up and secure with two wooden cocktail sticks. Cut the roll into two.
4. Place the rolls in a small container and pour in the cider.
5. Cover and cook on MEDIUM/50% for 4–6 minutes or until the pork is tender and the juices run clear when pierced with a skewer.
6. Allow to stand for 3 minutes before serving.

Bacon-Topped Potato   *L/M Easy*
Total cooking time: about 8 mins.

The flavour of the bacon seeps into the potato. Choose a
container into which the chop will fit snugly.

Ingredients
175g (6 oz) potato, thinly sliced
2–3 spring onions, chopped
ground black pepper
10ml (2 tsp) chopped parsley
15ml (1 tbsp) stock, cider or water
1 bacon chop

Method
1. In a small deep bowl, layer the potato and onions,
    seasoning the layers with black pepper and half the
    parsley.
2. Add the stock, cider or water and place the bacon
    chop on top. Cover and cook on HIGH for 6–8 minutes
    or until the potato is cooked in the centre – test with a
    skewer or sharp knife.
3. Sprinkle with the remaining parsley and allow the
    dish to stand, covered, for 3–5 minutes before
    serving.

Somerset Bacon   *L/M Easy*
Total cooking time: about 7 mins.

Choose a bacon chop with little fat. Vary the base by
using alternative vegetables, if wished.

Ingredients
1 leek, chopped
1 carrot, cut into thin fingers
pinch of dried sage
60ml (4 tbsp) apple juice or dry cider

ground black pepper
1 bacon chop

Method
1. Cook the leek, carrot, sage, apple juice and black pepper in a small covered container on HIGH for 3 minutes. Stir well.
2. Place the bacon chop on top of the vegetables, cover and cook on HIGH for 3–4 minutes.
3. Allow the dish to stand, covered, for about 3 minutes before serving.

Bacon Hash   *S/L Easy*
                                Total cooking time: about 10 mins.

Make Corned Beef Hash by omitting the bacon and stirring in 50–75g (2–3 oz) flaked corned beef at stage 6.

Ingredients
225g (8 oz) potatoes, cut into chunks
2 spring onions, chopped
30ml (2 tbsp) water
2 rashers of bacon
15g (½ oz) butter
salt and ground black pepper
25g (1 oz) cheese, grated

Method
1. Put the potatoes in a container with the onions and water.
2. Cover and cook on HIGH for 5–6 minutes until just tender, stirring once during cooking.
3. Allow the potatoes to stand for a few minutes while you cook the bacon.
4. Place the bacon rashers on a microwave rack. Cook on HIGH for 3 minutes or until the rashers are just beginning to crispen.

5. Mash the potatoes with the onions and their cooking
    water and the butter (use a fork for ease). Season to
    taste.
6. Cut the bacon into small pieces and stir these into the
    potato.
7. Place the mixture in a serving dish, sprinkle with
    cheese and cook on HIGH for 1 minute. Alternatively,
    brown the surface under a hot grill if the container is
    suitable.

Curried Chicken

L/M Easy
Total cooking time: about 11 mins.

Skin the chicken joint for this recipe if preferred. Serve
with rice and a salad of tomato, onion and lemon juice.

Ingredients
350g (12 oz) chicken joint
1.25ml (¼ tsp) ground cumin
1.25ml (¼ tsp) ground coriander
1 small onion, chopped
1 garlic clove, crushed (optional)
5ml (1 tsp) vegetable oil
5ml (1 tsp) curry paste
pinch of turmeric
45ml (3 tbsp) natural yoghurt
5ml (1 tsp) tomato purée
45ml (3 tbsp) water
salt and ground black pepper
15g (½ oz) creamed coconut, grated

Method
1. Place the chicken in a container, sprinkle the cumin
    and coriander over, cover and cook on HIGH for 5–6
    minutes, or until the juices run clear when the
    thickest part of the chicken is pierced with a skewer.
    Allow it to stand, covered for 5 minutes.

2. In another covered container cook the onion, garlic, oil, curry paste and turmeric on HIGH for 2 minutes.
3. Stir in the yoghurt, tomato purée, water, salt and pepper and cook, covered, on HIGH for a further 2 minutes.
4. Stir in the creamed coconut and pour the sauce over the chicken and its juices.
5. Cook uncovered on HIGH for 1 minute and serve.

Spicy Chicken Drumsticks

L/M Easy
Total cooking time: about 6 mins.

Remove the chicken skin if you like. Serve with rice and salad – delicious! Good served cold too!

Ingredients
15ml (1 tbsp) tomato purée
10ml (2 tsp) French mustard
pinch of chilli powder
salt and ground black pepper
2 chicken drumsticks

Method
1. Mix together the first four ingredients.
2. Brush the drumsticks with the mixture and arrange them on a microwave rack on a plate – thin ends to the middle, or thin ends overlapping to encourage even cooking.
3. Cover with a sheet of greaseproof paper and cook on HIGH for 4–6 minutes or until the juices run clear when the chicken is pierced with a skewer.
4. Allow the chicken to stand for about 3 minutes before serving.

Chicken in Red Wine

M Easy
Total cooking time: about 20 mins.

This classic dish is no longer a chore to prepare in small quantities.

Ingredients
2 chicken drumsticks
100g (4 oz) baby onions
1 rasher of bacon, rindless, chopped
pinch of ground cloves
pinch of garlic granules
15ml (1 tbsp) plain flour
7.5ml (½ tbsp) tomato purée
15ml (1 tbsp) brandy (optional)
150ml (¼ pt) red wine
pinch of mixed dried herbs
salt and ground black pepper
50g (2 oz) button mushrooms

Method
1. Arrange the drumsticks on a rack on a plate, thinner ends to the centre, or overlapping. Cover and cook on HIGH for 4–6 minutes or until the juices run clear when the drumsticks are pierced with a skewer.
2. Pour the chicken juices into a bowl and add the onions, bacon, cloves and garlic. Cover and cook on HIGH for 3 minutes.
3. Stir in the flour, then blend in the tomato purée, brandy (optional), wine, mixed herbs and seasoning. Cover and cook for 3 minutes, stirring every minute until boiling.
4. Add the drumsticks and mushrooms, cover and cook on DEFROST/30% for about 8 minutes or until the chicken is tender, stirring once or twice.

Liver Stir-Fry *L/M Easy*
Total cooking time: about 5 mins.

The speedy cooking of the microwave suits this dish.

Ingredients
10ml (2 tsp) soy sauce
5ml (1 tsp) wine vinegar
5ml (1 tsp) sherry
good pinch of ground ginger
100g (4 oz) carrots, cut into 5cm (2 in) sticks
5ml (1 tsp) cornflour
salt and ground black pepper
100g (4 oz) lamb's liver, cut into thin 5cm (2 in) strips
½ red pepper, sliced
3 spring onions, cut into 5cm (2 in) lengths

Method
1. Place the first five ingredients into a container, cover and cook on HIGH for 1 minute.
2. Season the cornflour with salt and ground black pepper and use it to coat the liver slices (this is easy if flour and liver are put into a small plastic bag and shaken).
3. Stir the liver into the carrots, cover and cook on HIGH for 1 minute.
4. Stir in the pepper and spring onions, cover and cook on HIGH for 2–3 minutes, stirring once during cooking.
5. Allow to stand 2 minutes before serving.

Lemony Liver *L/M Easy*
Total cooking time: about 5 mins.

The liver is easy to slice into thin slivers if it is partially frozen. Serve this light dish with buttered rice or pasta.

Ingredients
15g (½ oz) butter (optional)
1 small onion, chopped
100g (4 oz) lamb's liver, sliced into thin slivers
salt and ground black pepper
15ml (1 tbsp) lemon juice
15ml (1 tbsp) chopped parsley

Method
1. Place the butter (optional) and onion into a container. Cover and cook on HIGH for 2 minutes.
2. Stir in the liver and cook on HIGH for about 3 minutes, stirring every minute, or until the liver is just cooked.
3. Season to taste, stir in the lemon juice and parsley, and allow it to stand, covered, for 3–5 minutes before serving.

Minty Lamb Skewers

L/M Easy
Total cooking time: about 5 mins.

Serve with plain yoghurt which has been flavoured with a little chopped mint. It is also delicious with tomato sauce on a bed of rice.

Ingredients
1 small slice of bread
175g (6 oz) lean minced lamb
salt and ground black pepper
30ml (2 tbsp) finely chopped mint
1 egg, size 3 or 4, beaten

Method
1. Grate the bread slice to make breadcrumbs.
2. Put all the ingredients into a bowl and mix well.
3. Using your hands, shape the mixture around two wooden skewers and lay them on a microwave rack on a plate.

4. Cover with kitchen paper and microwave on MEDIUM/ 50% for 5 minutes or more, turning them occasionally, until the lamb is cooked to your liking.
5. Allow them to stand for 3 minutes before serving.

Honeyed Lamb with Rosemary   *L/M Easy*
Total cooking time: about 4 mins.

The flavour of this dish is wonderful.

Ingredients
175g (6 oz) lamb chop
1 small garlic clove, sliced thinly
5ml (1 tsp) honey
5ml (1 tsp) soy sauce
1 sprig of rosemary, fresh
   OR 2.5ml (½ tsp) dried rosemary
ground black pepper

Method
1. Make a few slits in the chop and insert the garlic pieces. Place the chop in a small dish.
2. Mix together the honey and soy sauce and brush the mixture over the lamb. Lay (or sprinkle) the rosemary on top and season with black pepper.
3. Cover and cook on HIGH for about 4 minutes or until the lamb is cooked to your liking. Allow it to stand for 3–5 minutes before serving.

Tandoori Turkey   *L/M Easy*
Total cooking time: about 5 mins.

Flash the cooked turkey under a hot grill for a brown finish. Serve it with rice which has been cooked with turmeric or saffron.

Ingredients
45ml (3 tbsp) natural yoghurt
2 spring onions, chopped
½ garlic clove, crushed
small piece of root ginger, crushed
good pinch of chilli powder
2.5ml (½ tsp) paprika
2.5ml (½ tsp) garam masala
2.5ml (½ tsp) lemon or lime juice
175g (6 oz) turkey fillet

Method
1. Mix together all the ingredients except the turkey.
2. Make two or three slits in the turkey and pour the yoghurt mix over. Cover and allow it to marinade (in a cool place) for up to 2 hours.
3. Place the coated turkey on a microwave rack on a plate and cook uncovered on MEDIUM/50% for 4–5 minutes (or until the juices run clear when the turkey is pierced with a skewer).
4. Cover and allow the turkey to stand for 5 minutes before serving.

Duck with Fruity Sauce

M Needs a little extra care
Total cooking time: about 10 mins.

The redcurrant jelly may be replaced by the more conventional cherries or plums (use canned, drained and stoned). Alternatively use a thick, old-fashioned-style marmalade for a tangy orange sauce – and use orange juice instead of red wine.

Ingredients
350g (12 oz) duck joint
3–4 spring onions, chopped
knob of butter
25g (1 oz) button mushrooms, sliced thinly

pinch of mixed dried herbs
10ml (2 tsp) tomato purée
30ml (2 tbsp) redcurrant jelly
salt and ground black pepper
5ml (1 tsp) cornflour
30ml (2 tbsp) red wine or stock

Method
1. Place the duck on a microwave rack in a shallow container. Cover and cook for 2 minutes on HIGH.
2. Cover and continue cooking on DEFROST/30% for about 4 minutes then drain off any fat which has collected in the container.
3. Cover and continue cooking on DEFROST/30% for a further 2 minutes.
4. Drain off the fat and juice, cover and allow the duck to stand for 3–5 minutes.
5. Meanwhile place the onions, butter, mushrooms and mixed herbs in a small container, cover and cook on HIGH for 1 minute.
6. Stir in the remaining ingredients in the order listed then cook uncovered on HIGH for 1 minute or until thickened. Stir at least once during cooking.
7. Crisp the duck skin quickly under a hot grill before slicing it and spooning the sauce over.

11

VEGETABLES &
VEGETABLE DISHES

Vegetables cooked in the microwave retain maximum colour and flavour, and can be cooked to produce a texture which is soft or which has 'a bite' to suit your own preference. Small portions cook well in the microwave. Always use a container which leaves 2.5cm (1 in) headroom (no more). Small amounts of vegetables cooked in too large a container tend to dry up.

CHECKPOINTS FOR VEGETABLES
* Use good quality vegetables for good results.

* Personal taste will dictate cooking times – according to whether you like your vegetables with 'a bite' or whether you like them soft.

* 30 ml (2 tbsp) is sufficient water to cook most vegetables.

* Always cover vegetables during cooking to retain maximum moisture.

* Prick the skins of whole vegetables such as potatoes or courgettes, to prevent them bursting.

* Cut vegetables into small, even pieces for the best results.

* Stir or shake vegetables at least once during cooking.

* Salt vegetables after cooking or it will cause their surfaces to dry and toughen.

* When using microwave (or roasting) bags or boil-in-the-bags, tie them loosely or pierce them in a convenient place to allow steam to escape.

* Generally, frozen vegetables need no thawing before cooking in the microwave.

Cooking and standing should be completed in a small covered container or in a small roasting/microwave/boil-in-the-bag. Rearrange, stir or shake vegetables halfway through cooking for best results. If wished, add salt after cooking and before standing.

FRESH VEGETABLES
The chart overleaf gives suitable quantities of vegetables for a single portion with cooking and standing times.

Guide to cooking times

Vegetable	Amount	Water to add	Mins. on HIGH	Standing (mins.)
Artichoke:				
globe	1	30ml (2 tbsp)	4–6	3–4
Jerusalem	100g (4 oz)	15ml (1 tbsp)	3–4	3
Asparagus	100g (4 oz)	15ml (1 tbsp)	3	3–4
Aubergine	1 small, cubed	30ml (2 tbsp)	2–3	3
Beans:				
broad	100g (4 oz)	30ml (2 tbsp)	3–4	3
runner	100g (4 oz)	30ml (2 tbsp)	3–4	3
whole	100g (4 oz)	30ml (2 tbsp)	3–5	3–5
Beansprouts	75g (3 oz)	knob of butter	1–2	2–3
Beetroot	1 medium	to cover	5–6	5
Broccoli	100g (4 oz), small florets	45ml (3 tbsp)	3–5	5
Brussels sprouts	100g (4 oz)	30ml (2 tbsp)	2–4	3
Cabbage	100g (4 oz), shredded	15–30ml (1–2 tbsp)	3–4	3
Carrots	100g (4 oz), sliced	15–30ml (1–2 tbsp)	3–4	3
Cauliflower	100g (4 oz), florets	30ml (2 tbsp)	3	3
Celery	100g (4 oz)	30ml (2 tbsp)	3–4	3
Corn-on-the-cob	1	brush with melted butter	3	3–5
Courgettes	100g (4 oz)	15ml (1 tbsp)	3	3
Leeks	100g (4 oz)	15ml (1 tbsp)	3	3
Marrow	100g (4 oz), cubed	15ml (1 tbsp)	3	3
Mushrooms	50g (2 oz)	5ml (1 tsp) or knob of butter	1	1–2
Onions	1 medium, sliced	5ml (1 tsp) or knob of butter	2–3	2–3
	1 large, whole	15ml (1 tbsp)	2–2½	3–5
Parsnips	100g (4 oz)	15ml (1tbsp)	3	3
Peas	100g (4 oz)	15ml (1 tbsp)/ knob of butter	2–3	3
Potato: old	175g (6 oz): whole, pricked	—	5–6	5
	cubed	15ml (1 tbsp)	3	3
new	100g (4 oz)	15ml (1 tbsp)	2½–3½	3–5
Spinach	100g (4 oz)	shake off excess water	2–3	3
Swede	100g (4 oz), cubed	15ml (1 tbsp)	4–5	3–5
Tomato	1 large	butter knob, if liked	1–1½	2
Turnips	100g (4 oz)	30ml (2 tbsp)	3–5	3

Courgettes, Greek-Style
L/M Easy
Total cooking time: about 10 mins.

This dish makes a meal in itself when sprinkled with plenty of grated cheese. As a vegetable accompaniment it is delicious served hot or cold with meat or fish.

Ingredients
15g (½ oz) butter or margarine
100g (4 oz) courgettes, sliced
½ garlic clove, crushed
230g can of tomatoes, chopped
25g (1 oz) mushrooms, sliced
salt and ground black pepper
5ml (1 tsp) fresh oregano, chopped
** OR 2.5ml (½ tsp) dried oregano**

Method
1. Melt the butter or margarine on HIGH for 20–30 seconds.
2. Stir in the courgettes and garlic, cover and cook on HIGH for 2 minutes then stir well.
3. Add the remaining ingredients, stir well, cover and cook on HIGH for 6–8 minutes. Stir once during cooking.
4. Allow to stand, covered, for 5 minutes before serving.

Mushrooms à la Greque
S/L/M Easy
Total cooking time: about 3 mins.

This is delicious as a snack on toast or as a starter with crunchy French bread or croûtons.

Ingredients
100g (4 oz) button mushrooms
230g can of chopped tomatoes *(continued overleaf)*

(Mushrooms à la Greque continued)
5ml (1 tsp) cornflour
pinch of garlic granules
pinch of sugar
½ bay leaf, crushed
pinch of dried basil
salt and ground black pepper

Method
1.   Cook all the ingredients in a covered container on HIGH for 2 minutes, stirring halfway through cooking.
2.   Taste the sauce to check that the cornflour is cooked. If it still tastes 'starchy' microwave for a further ½–1 minute on HIGH.

Tasty Layered Potato

S/L/M Easy
Total cooking time: about 7 mins.

This dish tastes better if the potatoes are scrubbed and the peel is left on. A sprinkling of grated cheese added at stage 5 makes it a meal in itself.

Ingredients
175g (6 oz) potatoes, scrubbed and finely sliced
1 small onion, finely sliced
salt and ground black pepper
2.5ml (½ tsp) dried dill
30ml (2 tbsp) milk
15g (½ oz) butter or margarine

Method
1.   Arrange layers of potatoes and onion, alternately, in a small deep container, seasoning each layer with salt and pepper and dill. Finish with a layer of potatoes.
2.   Spoon the milk over the potatoes.
3.   In a small container melt the butter (optional) on

HIGH for 15–30 seconds and then brush it over the top of the potatoes.
4. Cover and cook on HIGH for about 6 minutes or until the potatoes feel soft when pierced with a knife.
5. If the container is suitable, brown the top of the potatoes under a hot grill.

Stuffed Pepper with Cheese   *L/M Easy*
Total cooking time: about 5 mins.

Here is a basic recipe for stuffed peppers. Vary the ingredients to suit your taste.

Ingredients
150g (5 oz) red, green or yellow pepper, halved lengthways and seeds removed
50g (2 oz) rice, cooked (see page 107)
1 spring onion, chopped
15g (½ oz) sultanas
25g (1 oz) mature cheese, grated
15ml (1 tbsp) natural yoghurt
1.25ml (¼ tsp) mixed spice
5ml (1 tsp) French mustard
salt and ground black pepper

Method
1. Place the pepper halves in a container and pour 15ml (1 tbsp) water around. Cover and cook on HIGH for 2 minutes.
2. Mix together the remaining ingredients and use the mixture to fill the pepper halves.
3. Cover and cook on HIGH for about 3 minutes or until the filling is heated through.

Vegetable Casserole   *L/M Easy*
                              Total cooking time: about 15 mins.

Vary the vegetable mixture according to the season. Try it using frozen vegetables too.

Ingredients
15g (½ oz) butter or margarine
1 small onion, thinly sliced
10ml (2 tsp) flour
1.25ml (¼ tsp) grated nutmeg
150ml (¼ pt) stock, chicken or vegetable (see page 42)
   or a mixture of stock and milk
40g (1½ oz) cheese, grated
salt and ground black pepper
110g (4 oz) potatoes, thinly sliced
1 small carrot, thinly sliced
25g (1 oz) peas
1 tomato, sliced

Method
1. Cook the butter on HIGH in a small bowl for 30 seconds or until melted.
2. Stir in the onion, cover and cook on HIGH for 1 minute until soft.
3. Stir in the flour, nutmeg and stock. Cook on HIGH, for about 3 minutes stirring once or twice, until the sauce thickens and boils.
4. Stir in the cheese and season to taste.
5. In a small container, layer the potatoes, carrot, peas and tomato (save one tomato slice to garnish) and top them with the sauce.
6. Cook uncovered on MEDIUM–HIGH/75% for about 10 minutes or until the potatoes are cooked in the centre (use a knife to test).
7. Allow the dish to stand for 3–5 minutes before garnishing with the tomato slice and serving.

Onion with Stilton and Walnuts   *S/L/M Easy*
Total cooking time: about 4 mins. + grilling

This dish really needs grilling to give it an attractive appearance, so use a flameproof container.

Ingredients
1 medium onion, roughly chopped
5ml (1 tsp) water
½ apple, cored and sliced
15ml (1 tbsp) chopped walnuts
ground black pepper
15–25g (½–1 oz) Stilton cheese, crumbled

Method
1. Place the onion in a small container with the water, cover and cook on HIGH for 3 minutes, stirring once during cooking.
2. Allow the onion to stand for 2–3 minutes before draining off the liquid and mixing in the apple, walnuts and black pepper.
3. Sprinkle the crumbled Stilton over the top and cook on HIGH for 1 minute.
4. Brown under a hot grill before serving.

Cheesy Broccoli   *L/M Easy*
Total cooking time: about 7 mins.

Omit the ham and add extra cheese to make it a meatless dish.

Ingredients
100g (4 oz) broccoli, cut into small florets
30ml (2 tbsp) water   *(continued overleaf)*

(Cheesy Broccoli continued)
15g (½ oz) flour
150ml (¼ pt) milk
15g (½ oz) butter
2.5ml (½ tsp) mustard, prepared
1 slice of ham, cut into thin strips
15ml (1 tbsp) grated Parmesan cheese
ground black pepper

Method
1. Place the broccoli in a small container, add the water, cover and cook on HIGH for about 4 minutes, stirring once, or until it is just cooked.
2. Allow the broccoli to stand while you make the sauce.
3. Place the flour in a jug and gradually stir in the milk. Add the butter and mustard and cook on HIGH for 2–3 minutes, stirring frequently until the sauce thickens and boils.
4. Stir in the ham, cheese (save a little for sprinkling over the finished surface) and seasoning.
5. Drain the broccoli and pour the sauce over it. Sprinkle with the remaining cheese and brown under a hot grill if liked (make sure the container is suitable).

Gingered Cabbage

L/M Easy
Total cooking time: about 5 mins.

Use fresh, chopped root ginger if you wish. Take care that it does not 'lump together' in one piece. Add some chopped crispy bacon to add 'bite'. Use the rest of the cabbage to make Cabbage with Ham and Yoghurt on page 97.

Ingredients
15g (½ oz) butter
100g (4 oz) cabbage, shredded
1.25ml (¼ tsp) ground ginger
salt and ground black pepper

Method
1. Melt the butter on HIGH for about 30 seconds.
2. Stir in the cabbage and ginger, cover and cook on HIGH for about 4 minutes, stirring once, or until the cabbage is just cooked.
3. Season to taste and allow the dish to stand, covered, for 3 minutes before serving.

Baked Vegetables

L/M Easy
Total cooking time: about 6 mins.

Use courgettes or parsnips in this recipe to ring the changes.

Ingredients
1 small carrot, sliced
1 stick of celery, sliced
1 spring onion, chopped
few small florets of cauliflower
pinch of fennel seeds
10ml (2 tsp) water
10ml (2 tsp) lemon juice
salt and ground black pepper
25g (1 oz) cheese, grated

Method
1. Place the vegetables in a container, sprinkle with the fennel seeds and pour the water and lemon juice over them.

2. Cover and cook on HIGH for about 5 minutes, stirring or shaking once or twice, or until the vegetables are just cooked.
3. Allow them to stand for 3 minutes before draining off the liquid. Season to taste and sprinkle the cheese over.
4. Either cook on HIGH for ½–1 minute until the cheese has melted,

or

if the dish is suitable, lightly brown the cheese topping under a hot grill.

Corn-on-the-cob with Garlic   *S/L/M Easy*
Butter   *Total cooking time: about 7 mins.*

The quantity of butter can be varied according to taste.

Ingredients
25g (1 oz) butter
1 garlic clove, crushed
1 medium cob of corn
5ml (1 tsp) chopped parsley or other fresh herb

Method
1. Place half the butter with the crushed garlic in a small container and cook on HIGH for 30 seconds or until melted.
2. Brush the butter over the corn then wrap it in non-stick or greaseproof paper.
3. Place the parcel on a plate and cook on HIGH for 5–6 minutes, turning it over half way through cooking, or until cooked.
4. Sprinkle the parsley over and allow the corn to stand for 3 minutes before melting the remaining butter over the top and serving it.

Savoury Stuffed Tomato

L/M Easy
Total cooking time: about 4 mins.

Try using left-over cooked rice, bulgar wheat, couscous or pulses to replace the bran flakes.

Ingredients
1 beef tomato
4 spring onions, chopped
pinch of garlic granules
5ml (1 tsp) vegetable oil
½ green pepper, chopped
15g (½ oz) raisins
15g (½ oz) chopped walnuts
1.25–2.5ml (¼–½ tsp) garam masala or curry powder
dash of Worcestershire sauce
15g (½ oz) bran flakes
salt and ground black pepper

Method
1. Slice the top off the tomato and scoop out the centre. Chop the contents.
2. Place the spring onions, garlic, vegetable oil, pepper and raisins into a bowl. Cover and cook on HIGH for 2 minutes.
3. Stir in the remaining ingredients and the chopped tomato and cook on HIGH for 1 minute.
4. Pile the mixture back into the tomato and replace its lid.
5. Place the stuffed tomato on a plate and cook on HIGH for 1 minute.
6. Allow to stand for 2 minutes, covered, before serving.

Spinach and Cheese Stuffed Potato   *L/M Easy*
Total cooking time: about 12 mins.

The jacket potato makes one of the speediest meals for one. The addition of spinach and cheese makes it a substantial meal.

Ingredients
225g (8 oz) potato, scrubbed and pricked
100g (4 oz) frozen spinach
25g (1 oz) butter or margarine
salt and ground black pepper
25g (1 oz) Cheddar cheese, grated
30ml (2 tbsp) natural yoghurt
5ml (1 tsp) chopped parsley
5ml (1 tsp) chopped chives
pinch of grated nutmeg

Method
1. Cook the potato on HIGH for 6–7 minutes until just tender. Halfway through cooking, turn it over. Stand for 5 minutes.
2. Cook the spinach in a covered container on HIGH for 5 minutes, stirring halfway through cooking. Drain well, stir in half the butter or margarine and season with salt and black pepper to taste.
3. Cut the potato in half lengthways and scoop out the flesh.
4. Mash the scooped-out potato with the rest of the butter or margarine and stir in the cheese, yoghurt, parsley, chives, nutmeg and seasoning.
5. Pile the mixture back into the potato halves and sit them on the bed of spinach to serve.

Cabbage with Ham and Yoghurt   *L/M Easy*
Total cooking time: about 5 mins.

Use the rest of the cabbage to make Gingered Cabbage on page 92. Use soured cream or smetana instead of yoghurt if liked.

Ingredients
15g (½ oz) butter
100g (4 oz) cabbage, shredded
3 spring onions, chopped
salt
1.25ml (¼ tsp) paprika
25g (1 oz) ham, chopped
15–30ml (1–2 tbsp) natural yoghurt

Method
1. Melt the butter on HIGH for about 30 seconds.
2. Stir in the cabbage and spring onions, cover and cook on HIGH for 3–4 minutes, stirring once, or until the cabbage is just cooked.
3. Season with salt and paprika and stir in the ham. Cover and cook on HIGH for 30 seconds.
4. Allow the cabbage to stand, covered, for 3 minutes before serving, topped with the yoghurt.

Minted Peas   *L/M Easy*
Total cooking time: about 3 mins.

A simple way to cheer up an everyday frozen vegetable. It is also good with a few leaves of shredded lettuce added at stage 2.

Ingredients
100g (4 oz) frozen peas
15ml (1 tbsp) double cream
5ml (1 tsp) mint sauce, ready made

Method
1. Cook the peas in a small covered bowl on HIGH for 2 minutes.
2. Stir in the cream and mint sauce, cover and cook for a further 1 minute.

12

CHEESE & EGGS

Cheese and egg dishes can easily overcook and become hard or stringy during any form of cooking. For this reason it is a good idea to melt cheese in the microwave on DEFROST/30%.

Eggs can be poached (see Breakfast section, page 34), scrambled, baked and made into omelettes in the microwave, but do not attempt to cook an egg in its shell. It can be positively dangerous as the shell explodes! Always remember to pierce the thin skin on egg yolks too, to prevent them from bursting open.

Cheese-Topped Baked Eggs   *S/L Easy*
          Total cooking time: about 1½ mins. + grilling

A simple, delicious dish served with wholewheat or granary bread. Use the grill to achieve a perfect finish – make sure your containers are flameproof.

Ingredients
2 eggs, size 2
1.25ml (¼ tsp) dried dill
salt and ground black pepper
25g (1 oz) Cheddar or Gruyère Cheese, grated

Method
1. Break the eggs into two ramekins or small dishes and pierce the yolks.
2. Sprinkle the dill over each egg and cook both containers on MEDIUM/50% for 1–1½ minutes or until the eggs are slightly undercooked.
3. Season to taste with salt and pepper and sprinkle the grated cheese over the eggs.
4. Place under a hot grill until the cheese bubbles then serve immediately.

Egg and Leek Bake

S/L Easy
Total cooking time: about 5 mins.

Another dish suitable for serving with wholewheat or granary bread.

Ingredients
1 small leek, chopped finely
knob of butter or margarine
2 eggs, size 2 or 3, beaten
pinch of ground mace
salt and ground black pepper
10ml (2 tsp) chopped chives

Method
1. Place the leek and butter in a small shallow container, cover and cook on HIGH for 2–3 minutes.
2. Mix the beaten eggs with the mace and seasoning to taste.

3. Pour the egg mixture over the leeks, cover with kitchen paper and cook on MEDIUM/50% for 1½–2 minutes or until the eggs are just set.
4. Sprinkle with chives and allow the eggs to stand covered for 2 minutes before serving.

Scrambled Eggs with Herb and Garlic Cheese

S/L Easy
Total cooking time: about 3 mins.

Use a ready-flavoured cream cheese for this recipe or mix plain cream cheese with your favourite herbs and some crushed garlic.

Ingredients
2 eggs, size 2, beaten
salt and ground black pepper
15ml (1 tbsp) milk
15g (½ oz) butter or margarine
40g (1½ oz) cream cheese with herbs and garlic

Method
1. Mix together the eggs, seasoning, milk and butter in a bowl and cook on HIGH for 1 minute, stirring halfway through cooking.
2. Crumble in the cream cheese and continue cooking on HIGH for 1–2 minutes, stirring every 30 seconds until the creamy mixture is almost cooked.
3. Allow the eggs to stand covered for 1 minute – they will set during this time.

Srambled Eggs with Mushroom and Cheese

S/L Easy
Total cooking time: 2–3½ mins.

Simply serve on toast.

Ingredients
50g (2 oz) button mushrooms, sliced
15g (½ oz) butter or margarine
2 eggs, size 2, beaten
15ml (1 tbsp) milk
salt and ground black pepper
25g (1 oz) cheese, grated
5ml (1 oz) chopped chives

Method
1. Place the mushrooms and butter in a bowl, cover and cook on HIGH for 1 minute.
2. Mix together the eggs, milk and seasoning and pour over the mushrooms.
3. Cook on HIGH for 1–2 minutes, stirring every 30 seconds until the egg is slightly undercooked.
4. Stir in the grated cheese and chives and cook on HIGH for a further 30 seconds.
5. Allow to stand covered for 1 minute before serving.

Spinach-filled Omelette   *S/L Easy*
Total cooking time: about 7 mins.

Spinach and eggs make good partners. The nutmeg adds a special flavour to the filling. Instead of nutmeg you could add a good sprinkling of Parmesan cheese.

Ingredients
50g (2 oz) frozen spinach
15g (½ oz) butter
salt and ground black pepper
pinch of nutmeg
2 eggs, size 2 or 3, beaten
30ml (2 tbsp) milk

Method
1. In a small covered container, cook the spinach on

HIGH for 4 minutes. Stir well, drain off the liquid, stir in half the butter and season with salt, black pepper and nutmeg.

2. In an 18cm (7 in) shallow round container, melt the rest of the butter on HIGH for 30 seconds. Tilt the container to spread the butter over its base.

3. Mix together the eggs and milk with a little seasoning and pour the mixture over the butter.

4. Cook the eggs on HIGH for 1 minute, then lift the cooked edges from the side of the container, moving them to the middle. Continue cooking for 1–2 minutes, moving the eggs every 30 seconds until they are nearly cooked.

5. Allow the eggs to stand covered for 1 minute before spreading the spinach over one side of the omelette and folding the other half over it.

Welsh Rarebit

S/L Easy
Total cooking time: about 2 mins.

It is preferable to heat the cheese mixture separately, then pour it onto freshly toasted bread. For a change, add some chopped spring onions.

Ingredients
50g (2 oz) cheese, grated
15ml (1 tbsp) brown ale
1.25ml (¼ tsp) mustard powder
knob of butter
salt and ground black pepper
1 slice of toasted bread, hot

Method
1. Mix together the cheese, brown ale, mustard, butter and seasoning.
2. Cook on MEDIUM/50% for about 2 minutes or until melted and hot. Stir once or twice during heating.

3.   Pour the mixture over the hot toast and serve immediately.

Quick Egg Florentine
S/L/M Easy
Total cooking time: about 5 mins.

Use a mature cheese for this recipe for the best flavour.

Ingredients
100g (4 oz) frozen chopped spinach
25g (1 oz) mature Cheddar cheese, grated
1 egg, size 2 or 3
ground black pepper
crusty bread, to serve

Method
1.   Place the spinach in a small shallow container, cover and cook on HIGH for 2–3 minutes. Drain.
2.   Sprinkle the cheese over the spinach then carefully break the eggs on the top. Prick the yolk.
3.   Cover and cook on MEDIUM/50% for 2–3 minutes or until the egg is just set.
4.   Season well with black pepper and serve with crusty fresh bread.

Warm Cheese Roll
L Easy
Total cooking time: about 1 min.

Sandwiches need not be served cold, particularly if they contain cheese. Use the microwave to warm the bread and melt the cheese. A little salad vegetable and/or some fruit adds to the interest. Try replacing the nectarine with grated apple or pickle.

Ingredients
1 large crusty roll
1 crisp lettuce leaf, such as Little Gem
1 small ripe nectarine or peach, peeled, stoned and sliced
50g (2 oz) Cheddar or Camembert cheese, thinly sliced
5–10ml (1–2 tsp) oil-and-vinegar dressing

Method
1. Halve the roll and place the lettuce on one half. Arrange the nectarine or peach on the lettuce, then the cheese slices on top. Drizzle the oil-and-vinegar dressing over and top with the other half of the roll.
2. Wrap the roll in greaseproof paper and cook on HIGH for ½–1 minute until just warmed through.

13

PASTA & RICE
& PIZZAS

Pasta and rice both cook well in the microwave, particularly in small quantities. There is not a great time-saving and they take the same time to cook, no matter what the quantity. However, convenience makes it a worthwhile method. Pasta and rice reheat superbly in the microwave too. There may be occasions, when you wish to save time, when you will want to cook the pasta on the hob while a sauce is being prepared in the microwave – or vice versa. Always add boiling water to the pasta or rice. A little cooking oil in the water helps to prevent them boiling over.

Pizzas are successful in the microwave too, particularly if cooked on a browning dish. See page 114 for details.

General method for pasta
1.   Place 75g (3 oz) pasta shapes (or spaghetti, broken to fit the container) in a deep container.

2. Stir in 2.5–5ml (½–1 tsp) vegetable oil and salt to taste.
3. Pour 900ml (1½ pt) boiling water over the pasta and stir well.
4. Cook uncovered on HIGH for 7–10 minutes (a little longer for wholewheat pasta), stirring occasionally, or until the pasta is just slightly undercooked.
5. Cover and allow it to stand for 3–5 minutes, until cooked to your liking, before draining and using.

General method for rice
1. Place 50g (2 oz) long grain rice in a deep container and stir in 2.5–5ml (½–1 tsp) vegetable oil and salt to taste.
2. Pour over 200ml (7 fl oz) boiling water and stir.
3. Cover loosely and cook on HIGH for 8–9 minutes. Do not stir.
4. Allow the rice to stand covered for 5 minutes until any remaining water has been absorbed. Fluff up with a fork and serve.

Brown rice: may need an extra 75ml (3 fl oz) boiling water and an extra 10 minutes cooking time.

Cannelloni

L/M Needs a little extra care
Total cooking time: about 9 mins.

This recipe uses cheese and spinach to fill the cannelloni tubes. Try it with the Bolognese sauce on page 67. Use fresh or cooked lasagne sheets to roll around the filling if you cannot get cannelloni tubes.

Ingredients
3 cannelloni tubes
5ml (1 tsp) vegetable oil
50g (2 oz) frozen spinach, thawed on DEFROST/30%
    for 2–3 minutes (and stand for 3 minutes), and drained
25g (1 oz) curd or cream cheese
good pinch of ground mace
salt and ground black pepper
3 spring onions, chopped
230g can of tomatoes, chopped
knob of butter or margarine
2.5–5ml (½–1 tsp) dried basil
25g (1 oz) Cheddar cheese, grated

Method
1. Place the cannelloni tubes and oil in a deep container, cover well with boiling water and cook on HIGH for 3–4 minutes, or until they are just soft.
2. Drain the cannelloni and allow them to cool in a damp tea towel.
3. Meanwhile mix together the spinach, curd or cream cheese and mace, seasoning well.
4. Fill the cannelloni tubes with this mixture and arrange them in a shallow dish.
5. Put the remaining ingredients (except the Cheddar cheese) into a small bowl, chopping the tomatoes into their juice. Cover and cook on HIGH for 3 minutes.
6. Season the tomato sauce with salt and ground black pepper and pour it over the cannelloni. Sprinkle with the Cheddar cheese and cook uncovered on HIGH for 1–2 minutes or until the cheese melts.

Pasta with Devilled   *S/L/M Easy*
Chicken Livers   *Total cooking time: about 8 mins.*

This chicken liver mixture is also delicious with rice or on toast.

Ingredients
50g (2 oz) small pasta shapes
2.5–5ml (½–1 tsp) vegetable oil
600ml (1 pt) water, boiling
5ml (1 tsp) sherry
5ml (1 tsp) Worcestershire sauce
2 drops Tabasco sauce
10ml (2 tsp) tomato purée
5ml (1 tsp) whole grain mustard
2.5ml (½ tsp) dried tarragon
ground black pepper
100g (4 oz) chicken livers, cut into 2.5cm (1 in) pieces
50g (2 oz) button mushrooms, sliced
25g (1 oz) seedless grapes, halved

Method
1. Put the pasta into a deep container with the oil. Pour the boiling water over it and cook uncovered on HIGH for 5 minutes, stirring once.
2. Allow the pasta to stand while you prepare the livers.
3. Mix together the sherry, Worcestershire sauce, tabasco, tomato purée, mustard, tarragon and pepper.
4. Stir in the chicken livers, cover and cook on MEDIUM/ 50% for 1½ minutes.
5. Stir in the mushrooms, cover and cook on MEDIUM/ 50% for a further 1½ minutes.
6. Stir in the grapes, cover and allow the dish to stand for 2 minutes.
7. Drain the pasta, stir in the devilled chicken livers and serve.

Tagliatelli with Creamy Cheese and Nut Sauce

L/M Easy
Total cooking time: about 6 mins.

Instead of freshly crushed garlic and herbs, try using the ready-made cream cheese with garlic and herbs added. Use low-fat cheese and low-fat yoghurt if you wish.

Ingredients
50g (2 oz) green tagliatelli
2.5–5ml (½–1 tsp) vegetable oil
600ml (1 pt) water, boiling
45ml (3 tbsp) soft cheese, such as curd or quark
1 spring onion, finely chopped
10ml (2 tsp) chopped parsley
1–2 garlic clove(s), crushed
10ml (2 tsp) dried basil
15ml (1 tbsp) chopped nuts, such as walnuts
10ml (2 tbsp) cream or yoghurt
ground black pepper

Method
1. Place the pasta and oil in a deep container and pour the boiling water over it. Cook uncovered on HIGH for 5–6 minutes or until the pasta is just cooked, stirring once. Allow to stand.
2. Meanwhile mix together the remaining ingredients in a separate bowl.
3. Drain the tagliatelli, stir in the sauce and serve.

Vegetable Pasta

L/M Easy
Total cooking time: about 11 mins.

Serve this with hot garlic bread.

Ingredients
75g (3 oz) pasta shapes
4 spring onions, sliced
100g (4 oz) courgettes, sliced
50g (2 oz) celery, sliced
1 vegetable stock cube
100ml (4 fl oz) water, boiling
10ml (2 tsp) soy sauce
30ml (2 tbsp) single cream
salt and freshly ground black pepper
Parmesan or Cheddar cheese, grated, to serve

Method
1. Cook the pasta following the general method on page 106. Allow to stand while the sauce is made.
2. Put the onions, courgette and celery into a bowl. Dissolve the stock cube in the boiling water and stir into the vegetables.
3. Cover and cook on HIGH for 4 minutes, stirring halfway through cooking, or until just tender.
4. Drain the pasta and add the vegetables and their juice, the soy sauce and cream. Season to taste and serve, topped with cheese if wished.

Savoury Rice   *L/M Easy*
                        Total cooking time: about 10 mins.

Adding some cooked meat such as ham or chicken, or fish such as tuna or salmon, at stage 2 makes this a very substantial meal.

Ingredients
50g (2 oz) long grain rice
2.5ml (½ tsp) vegetable oil
200ml (7 fl oz) water, boiling   *(continued overleaf)*

(Savoury Rice continued)
1.25ml (¼ tsp) turmeric
2 spring onions, chopped
25g (1 oz) frozen peas
25g (1 oz) frozen sweetcorn
25g (1 oz) button mushrooms, sliced
15ml (1 tbsp) chopped parsley
salt and ground black pepper

Method
1. Place the rice and oil in a deep container and pour the boiling water over. Stir in the turmeric and cook uncovered on HIGH for 7 minutes.
2. Add the onions, peas, sweetcorn and mushrooms. Cover and cook on HIGH for a further 3 minutes.
3. Stir in the parsley and seasoning to taste, cover and allow the rice to stand for 3 minutes before serving.

Almond Risotto

L/M Easy
Total cooking time: about 20 mins.

This gives you the basic method for a risotto which, if you use an Italian-style rice, is deliciously creamy.

Ingredients
15g (½ oz) butter
1 small leek, thinly sliced
50g (2 oz) Arborio, risotto or long grain rice
300ml (½ pt) vegetable or chicken stock, boiling
60ml (4 tbsp) dry vermouth
50g (2 oz) button mushrooms
25g (1 oz) flaked almonds, toasted
grated Parmesan or mature Cheddar cheese, to taste

Method
1. Cook the butter in a bowl on HIGH for 30 seconds until melted.

2. Stir in the leek and rice. Cover and cook on HIGH for 1 minute.
3. Stir in the boiling stock and the vermouth.
4. Cook uncovered on HIGH for 2–3 minutes until boiling, then continue cooking on MEDIUM/50% for about 15 minutes until the rice is tender and it has absorbed all the stock.
5. Stir in the mushrooms and nuts and cook uncovered for 1 minute.
6. Serve, topped with cheese to taste.

Pizza-Topped Crumpets   *S/L/M Easy*
Total cooking time: about 2½ mins.

A deliciously quick pizza-style snack without the time-consuming method! Try this recipe with a halved muffin in place of the crumpets.

Ingredients
2 rashers of bacon
knob of butter or margarine
2 crumpets
1 tomato, sliced
1.25ml (¼ tsp) mixed dried herbs
salt and ground black pepper
30ml (2 tbsp) cheese, grated

Method
1. Place the bacon rashers on a microwave rack on a plate and cook on HIGH for 1 minute or until beginning to turn crisp.
2. Spread a little butter on each crumpet and place them on a plate.
3. Arrange the tomato slices on the crumpets and chop the bacon over them.
4. Sprinkle with the herbs and seasoning to taste.
5. Top with the grated cheese and cook on HIGH for 1–1½ minutes or until the cheese melts.

Personalised Pizzas   *S/L Easy*
Total cooking time: about 3 mins.

Keep packs of individual cheese and tomato pizzas in the
freezer. Add toppings to suit yourself – to make a snack
or substantial meal with a mixed salad. A browning dish
gives best results.

Topping suggestions
chopped green pepper and mushrooms
anchovies and black olives
lashings of fresh (or dried) herbs and extra cheese
crispy bacon and sweetcorn kernels
ham and mushrooms

Method
1. Pre-heat a browning dish on HIGH for about 4 minutes
    (check with the manufacturer's instructions).
2. Brush with 7.5–15ml (½–1 tbsp) vegetable oil then
    add the frozen pizza with its topping.
3. Cook on HIGH for about 3 minutes or until the cheese
    in the centre of the pizza bubbles.
4. Allow the pizza to stand on the hot browning dish for
    2–3 minutes before serving.

14

DESSERTS

With the microwave you can prepare individual puddings speedily and at little extra expense. Sponge, suet and fruit puddings, which would normally need hours of steaming conventionally, cook in minutes. Fruits cooked in the microwave are tender and remain beautifully whole. Remember to split the skin of whole fruit such as apples, and cut other fruits into equal-sized pieces to encourage even cooking.

Oranges in Caramel   *L/M Easy*
                              Total cooking time: about 5 mins.

A fresh fruit can be transformed with the help of the microwave.

Ingredients
45ml (3 tbsp) orange juice
5ml (1 tsp) rum (optional)   *(continued overleaf)*

(Oranges in Caramel continued)
7.5ml (½ tbsp) sultanas
25g (1 oz) caster sugar
45ml (3 tbsp) water
1 orange, seedless if possible

Method
1. Put the orange juice, rum (optional) and sultanas into a small bowl. Cover and cook on HIGH for 1 minute.
2. Put the sugar and water into another bowl and cook on HIGH for 1 minute. Stir well to dissolve the sugar completely.
3. Cook the sugar mixture again on HIGH, stirring every 30 seconds, until the syrup just turns a pale golden brown. (Take care not to burn it.)
4. Allow the syrup to cool for a few minutes before slowly adding the orange juice. Cook on HIGH for 30 seconds.
5. Peel the orange, removing the pith and any seeds. Slice and pour the syrup over the orange.
6. Serve hot or chilled.

Banana – Tropical Style   *S/L/M Easy*
                    Total cooking time: about 1½ mins.

Use a firm banana so that it keeps its shape.

Ingredients
1 banana, peeled, sliced thickly
5ml (1 tsp) lemon or lime juice
1 small orange, segmented
knob of butter or margarine
5–10ml (1–2 tsp) demerara sugar
10ml (2 tsp) desiccated coconut
15ml (1 tbsp) raisins
15ml (1 tbsp) pineapple juice

Method
1. Toss the banana slices in lemon or lime juice and mix them with the orange segments.
2. Add the butter or margarine. Mix together the remaining ingredients and add these too.
3. Cover and cook on HIGH for 1–1½ minutes. Serve hot.

Queen of Puddings

L/M Easy
Total cooking time: about 2½ mins.

This traditional pudding will not have a crisp finish. Sprinkle the meringue with chopped nuts to add crunch.

Ingredients
1 egg, size 3 or 4, separated
5ml (1 tsp) demerara sugar
knob of butter or margarine
75ml (3 fl oz) milk
2.5ml (½ tsp) grated lemon rind
75ml (5 tbsp) fresh breadcrumbs
30ml (2 tbsp) frozen raspberries, blackberries, gooseberries or plums
15ml (1 tbsp) caster sugar
7.5ml (½ tbsp) chopped walnuts or hazelnuts

Method
1. Mix together the egg yolk, demerara sugar, butter and milk, and cook uncovered on HIGH for 30 seconds.
2. Stir in the lemon rind and the breadcrumbs and spoon the mixture into a small dish.
3. Sprinkle the frozen fruit over the breadcrumb mix.
4. Whisk the egg white until stiff, then whisk in the caster sugar to make the meringue.
5. Spoon the meringue over the fruit, sprinkle it with

chopped nuts and cook uncovered on MEDIUM/50%
for about 2 minutes, until set.

Sponge Pudding with Jam Sauce   *L/M Easy*
Total cooking time: about 3 mins.

A mini version of everyone's favourite home-made pud!

Ingredients
40g (1½ oz) self-raising flour
25g (1 oz) soft margarine
25g (1 oz) caster sugar
1 egg, size 4 or 5, beaten
few drops of vanilla essence
10ml (2 tsp) milk
30ml (2 tbsp) jam
10ml (2 tsp) water
few drops of lemon juice

Method
1. Beat together the flour, margarine, sugar, egg,
   vanilla flavouring and milk until smooth.
2. Put the mixture into a small, lightly-greased bowl or
   teacup and smooth the top.
3. Cover loosely and cook on HIGH for 1½–2 minutes.
4. Remove the cover immediately and allow the pudding to stand for 2 minutes before turning it out.
5. Meanwhile cook the remaining ingredients in a small
   bowl or jug, on HIGH for 1 minute.
6. Stir the jam sauce well and pour it over the pudding.

Cinnamon Apple Crumble   *L/M Easy*
Total cooking time: about 1 min.

A deliciously quick pudding – serve with Greek yoghurt,
cream or custard flavoured with a little cinnamon.

Ingredients
1 eating apple, sliced
10ml (2 tsp) sultanas
15ml (1 tbsp) demerara sugar
pinch of ground cinnamon
2 crunchy biscuits, such as ginger or lemon cookies

Method
1. Arrange the apple in the base of a small dish and sprinkle the sultanas over.
2. Mix half the sugar with the cinnamon and sprinkle this over the apple.
3. Cover and cook on HIGH for 1 minute.
4. Crush the biscuits and mix them with the remaining sugar. Sprinkle this over the apple.
5. Cook uncovered on HIGH for ½–1 minute.

Pavlova For One   *L/M Easy*
                    Total cooking time: about 1–1¼ mins.

The proportion of sugar in this recipe is high enough to make this a once-in-a-while treat only. A conventional meringue mixture does not crisp up in the microwave.

Ingredients
10ml (2 tsp) egg white
about 25g (1 oz) icing sugar, sieved well
30ml (2 tbsp) double cream
45ml (3 tbsp) fresh fruit, such as halved black grapes and raspberries
2 squares of plain chocolate

Method
1. Break up the egg white with a fork.
2. Use a wooden or plastic spoon to mix in the icing sugar, a little at a time, until you have a fondant-like

paste which is thick enough to shape with your hands.

3. Divide the mixture into two pieces and flatten them into ½cm (¼ in) thick circles.

4. Place the circles on a large sheet of non-stick baking paper, leaving space between the two.

5. Cook on HIGH for about 1–1¼ minutes or until the meringue does not fall when the microwaves are switched off. If they do fall, simply switch the oven on again for a further few seconds. Take care not to overcook or the meringue will turn brown during its standing period (though a light caramel colour does give a beautiful flavour).

6. Allow the meringues to cool for a few minutes before carefully lifting them off the paper.

7. Whip the cream, spread it carefully over one meringue, sprinkle the fruit over and top with the second meringue.

8. In a small bowl, cook the chocolate on MEDIUM/50% for about 30 seconds or until melted. Use a teaspoon to dribble the chocolate over the top meringue.

Spotted Dick

L/M Easy
Total cooking time: about 3 mins.

Use the all-in-one-method to make this traditional pud in minutes. Softening the fruit first as in stage 1 below gives the best results.

Ingredients
5ml (1 tsp) water
25g (1 oz) currants
25g (1 oz) soft margarine
25g (1 oz) caster sugar
25g (1 oz) self-raising flour
1 egg, size 4, beaten
few drops of vanilla essence

Method
1. Place the water and currants in a small container, cover and cook on HIGH for about 45 seconds to plump up and soften the fruit.
2. Beat together the remaining ingredients until thoroughly mixed.
3. Lightly grease a cup or a small pudding basin.
4. Fold the currants and their liquid into the cake mixture and turn it into the prepared cup or basin.
5. Cook uncovered for 2–2½ minutes.
6. Allow the pudding to stand for 2 minutes before turning it out.

Orange Chocolate Pots
L/M Easy
Total cooking time: about 4 mins.

Always use the microwave to melt chocolate for a recipe. It is much simpler than the usual method using a bowl over a pan of boiling water.

Ingredients
50g (2 oz) orange chocolate cake covering
30ml (2 tbsp) double or whipping cream
1 egg white, size 1 or 2

Method
1. Break the chocolate into a bowl and cook on MEDIUM/50% for about 3 minutes, stirring once or twice, or until the chocolate has melted.
2. Allow the chocolate to cool slightly.
3. Whip the cream to soft peaks and fold in to the chocolate.
4. Whisk the egg white until it forms stiff peaks then fold it gently into the chocolate.
5. Turn the mixture into a glass or serving dish and chill for about 1 hour before serving.

Baked Egg Custard

L/M Easy
Total cooking time: about 6 mins.

A single baked egg custard is ready to eat in less than 15 minutes!

Ingredients
150ml (¼ pt) milk
1 egg, size 3, lightly beaten
5–10ml (1–2 tsp) caster sugar
drop of vanilla essence
grated nutmeg

Method
1. In a small jug, heat the milk on HIGH for 1 minute.
2. Mix together the egg, sugar and vanilla essence and lightly whisk in the warmed milk.
3. Strain the mixture into a small straight-sided container and sprinkle some grated nutmeg over it.
4. Cook uncovered on MEDIUM/50% for about 5 minutes or until just set.
5. Allow the custard to stand for 5 minutes before serving.

Pear with Melba Sauce

L/M Easy
Total cooking time: about 5 mins.

Treat yourself to this glamorous pud. The sauce can be served hot or cold. Use a ripe pear.

Ingredients
1 large pear, whole, peeled
30ml (2 tbsp) apple juice
10ml (2 tsp) caster sugar
2.5ml (½ tsp) cornflour
100g (4 oz) raspberries, fresh or frozen, defrosted on

**DEFROST/30% for 2 minutes (and stand for 3 minutes),
puréed or sieved**
2.5ml (½ tsp) lemon juice

Method
1. Place the pear in a small bowl with the apple juice, cover and cook on HIGH for 3 minutes or until the pear is just tender. Allow it to stand covered while the sauce is prepared.
2. In another small bowl or jug, mix together the sugar and cornflour with 10ml (2 tsp) water.
3. Stir in the raspberry purée and cook uncovered on HIGH for 1–2 minutes, stirring every 30 seconds, or until the sauce is thick.
4. Stir the lemon juice into the sauce.
5. Drain the liquid from the pear and add it to the sauce. Pour over the pear and serve.

Sweet White Sauce

S/L/M Easy
Total cooking time: about 3 mins.

Serve this with sponge and fruit puddings. Stir in a little single cream after stage 4 for special occasions.

Ingredients
15g (½ oz) butter
15g (½ oz) flour
150ml (¼ pt) milk
7.5–15ml (½–1 tbsp) caster sugar

Method
1. In a small bowl or jug, cook the butter on HIGH for 30 seconds or until melted.
2. Stir in the flour and gradually blend in the milk.
3. Cook on HIGH for 2–3 minutes, stirring every 30 seconds, until the sauce thickens, boils and rises up the sides of the container.

4. Stir in the sugar and allow the sauce to stand for 2
    minutes.

Brandy Sauce: Add 5ml (1 tsp) brandy after stage 4.

Chocolate Sauce: Stir in 15ml (1 tbsp) grated chocolate
with the sugar at stage 3.

Spicy Sauce: Add 1.25ml (¼ tsp) mixed spice at stage 2.

INDEX

Words and numbers in italics refer to actual recipes.

FREE
If you would like an up-to-date list of all **RIGHT WAY** titles currently available, please send a stamped self-addressed envelope to
ELLIOT RIGHT WAY BOOKS,
KINGSWOOD, SURREY, KT20 6TD, U.K.